CLOSE THAT DOOR

And Keep The Devil Out

by

Timothy McFall

Unless otherwise indicated, all Scripture quotations are taken from the *King James Version* of the Bible.

Close That Door And Keep The Devil Out
ISBN 0-9672308-0-2
Copyright © 1999 by Dr. Timothy McFall
P. O. Box 1902
Klamath Falls, OR 97601

Printed in the United States of America. All rights reserved under International Copyright Law. Contents and/or cover may not be reproduced in whole or in part in any form without the express written consent of the Publisher.

CONTENTS

Introduction

CHAPTER 1 Close That Door 9

CHAPTER 2 An Unsinkable Ship 21

CHAPTER 3 His Character — Your Character 33

CHAPTER 4 Stealing Is Stealing 43

CHAPTER 5 Deception 47

CHAPTER 6 Deception — Part II 53

CHAPTER 7 Stand, Therefore 63

CHAPTER 8 Chosen For Assignment 69

CHAPTER 9 Learning The Hard Way 77

CHAPTER 10 Giants In The Land 83

CHAPTER 11 Bolt The Door 95

CHAPTER 12 Never, Never Lie 101

FOREWORD

In every move of God, He raises up men and women of faith to speak and write truth into our hearts. I believe that Timothy McFall is such a man, anointed and called for this hour.

This book, written, I believe, under the anointing of the Holy Spirit, helps us to understand some of the simple truths of scripture and I know it will challenge you as it did me to *Close That Door* to all that the enemy attempts to steal from us.

Each chapter, fresh with humor and believability, is taken out of the experiences of Tim's life and ministry and is confirmed by reference to God's Word. Rarely, will an author give you such honest insight into his personal life and allow you the reader, to see the failures and triumphs in such transparency. Everyone who reads this book will laugh and cry as you identify with the author.

I have known the author now for several years and have had the pleasure to minister with him on a few occasions and he always has a fresh word form the Lord that blesses me. Knowing the author as I do enables me to say that you are about to receive some awesome growth information. God has gifted Tim in a wonderful way to assist you to overcome in the areas that Satan has tried to control.

In *Close That Door*, you will be challenged to move up to a higher level in your walk with the Lord. You'll learn that God never meant for you to struggle through life in defeat, but He is working in you to prepare you for the most abundant life you could ever imagine.

This is a book you will want to read more than once. So enjoy each page and savor the richness of the message.

Louise Brock

DEDICATION

I dedicate this book to my wife Donna Marie, who has always believed in me, loved me, helped me, and supported me spiritually, mentally and physically. Without her there would have been no book.

To my children, Darla McFall Parthemore and Terry Parthemore. To my children, Daniel and Kristin McFall.

Darla has always been a friend who I can talk to. Terry has always been a father-in-law's dream, who has had the strength and wisdom to help me turn the corners in ministry.

Daniel, who has given his life to help bring the vision from the Lord come to pass. Our relationship is more than a father and son relationship; it is also a friendship.

Kristin, who has given us two beautiful grandchildren who bring fulfillment to our lives.

Donna and I dedicate this book to our friends and partners who helped finance this book by underwriting the cost of a page or pages. This is your book. You will reap a harvest from its fruit.

ACKNOWLEDGMENTS

Thank you so very much to our church family at Jubilee Fellowship, Klamath Falls, Oregon. You have faithfully prayed and stood behind the vision the Lord gave us. You are a blessing.

Thank you also to Revs. Bruce and Christine Wingard who, through prayer and direction from our Lord Jesus, crafted the "coat of many colors" that is this book. Their calling from the Lord—Holy Ghostwriters—enables them to catch the revelation of the Spirit and bridge it from tape to paper without losing the anointing. Thank you for your prayers, your dedication and the hard work necessary to make this book a reality.

CHAPTER 1
CLOSE THAT DOOR

When I was in the military, I was sent for training to desensitize my emotions. That seems kind of odd in today's social climate where we do everything possible to make people sensitive to others, but, as usual, the army had a purpose all its own. The training took place immediately following a period in my service where everyone had been ugly and mean to me for the last three months.

I came into the training about half mad at everyone. This one day thirty of us were gathered together in a room and one of the guys was talking with several of us, asking where we were from, what kind of marriages we had, and if we had any children, and he was just so friendly. He was like a mug of hot chocolate on a frosty day; just kind of warmed my insides.

When he came across one of the fellows we called Tex, because he was from Texas, all of a sudden he turned mean. "You know everybody I ever met from Texas was stupid," he said. "In fact, I can't stand Texans." Then he started in about Tex's mother, and said some very uncomplimentary things. Tex jumped up to whip the guy, and two security guards had to wrestle him down to the ground.

At this point the fellow who had turned mean to Tex grinned real big and told us he was an instructor and this had all been a training

— 9 —

exercise. He let us know we were going to experience emotional feelings, but they would train us how to handle them so we wouldn't give in to them.

All the rest of us breathed a collective sigh of relief, but Tex didn't care if it was a training exercise or not. He just wanted to whip that instructor. The last time I saw Tex he was still looking for that guy, he still hadn't given up the training exercise. All he could say was, "That guy shouldn't have said what he did about my mother."

"Tex, get real," I said, "it was only a training exercise, he didn't mean it."

"I don't care. He should have chosen your mother, not mine."

The purpose of the training was to make us aware of how people can put pressure on you through your emotions. And if you're not aware of what you're experiencing, all you want to do is get out from under that pressure. The truth is most people, when the pressure gets great enough, will do anything to get out. Satan uses this tactic to sucker us into positions where he can gain a foothold in our lives.

I've been suckered into a lot of spiritual fights, haven't you? It's like my desensitivity training, if I had known I was being tested, I would have done much better. But the problem with a test is, you never know when one is coming. You can't see them up ahead. In James 1, God says that trials aren't something put on you, they are something that you fall into: *"My brethren, count it all joy when ye fall into divers temptations; knowing this, that the trying of your faith worketh patience"* (v.2,3). Now that word trying is like trial. We learn that in some way or another the temptation comes before the trial. We fall into the temptation and are thereby tried, or tested. We are tested by how we react to the temptation. God doesn't tempt us; He's not the tempter: *Let no man say when he is tempted, I am tempted of God: for God cannot be tempted with evil, neither tempteth he any man.* (James 1:13).

Okay, then if that's the case, how do temptations come? Keep reading and you will see.

SEASONS OF TEMPTATION

But every man is tempted, when he is drawn away of his own lust, and enticed. (James 1:14) A wrong understanding of this verse might lead someone whose temptation was whiskey to show up Sunday morning in church saying, "Whooo, I feel good! Glory, glory!"

"Why do you feel so good?"

"Well, I went out and I got drunk last night and the Bible says, **'Count it all joy when you fall into divers temptations'.**" However, that kind of temptation cannot be the kind to which James is making reference. No, he's talking about the things that tempt your faith. Things that lead you off the walk of faith. The problem of falling into temptations is, according to Matthew 6:13, if you're not being led of the Holy Ghost you will be led into temptations by the Devil.

Many times, I've been led right into the middle of some strife problem, not knowing it. You know, I passed up 14 chances to turn down strife, but number 15 caught me at the wrong time. I normally would not have yielded, but I yielded, because it got me at a time of weakness or unpreparedness; a bad time. Like a deer in October...I was in season.

Well, the Devil is smart enough to know the best time to show up is when you're in season. He knows when you are not in season for something. He doesn't try to use those certain things on you then, he waits, and says, *"Hey, boys, he's in season now, let's get him."* Like any good hunter, he knows when you are in season for certain temptations he can hope to get you to fall into. He sets the circumstance, the right amount of heat, the right amount of pressure within your family, the right amount of pressure within your job, and then you get in season to start to produce a crop of sin. Satan never just comes arbitrarily, he waits for and works on your seasons.

Now if somebody comes up and whops me across the arm with a big stick, I know I'm going to have a certain emotion. "Oh, man, that hurts. Whoa, that hurts. Hey, what's the matter with you? Don't hit me any more!"

But the same thing can happen in the emotional realm. Somebody can whop you up around the side of your feelings and your emotions, and if you don't know how to handle that, you can get suckered into a fight. Right?

I have a friend, and one time his little boy ran up to me and kicked me in the shins. I mean, he just hauled off and pasted me. He was about five years old. I'm telling you, in that moment I became grateful for all that training the service had given me. I was able to not show my emotions. So instead of hollering at the kid, "You little twerp, what's the matter with you?" I just stood there with the pain shooting up my leg trying to overtake me. I wanted to knock him into next week, but instead all I did was hold his shoulder to try to keep him away from me.

When he saw the first kick didn't effect me, he thought he was going to have to do it again, harder. I could see it in his face. Even though I had been trained not to show reaction, that didn't make the pain any less real. You might have a temptation kicking you in the shins, so to speak, but don't yield to it.

Satan also knows what or who to use to kick us. What can happen is baby Christians will run up and kick you right in the emotional shins and, if you're not careful, you'll want to do a body slam on them. I can see it now...you get kicked and then when you react the baby says, "Well I thought you walked in love?" All you can say then is, "Well, I did until I got in pain."

The Devil caught you in season. If we get in pain of some kind, and we're not careful, we will yield a pretty unhealthy crop of strife. Have you been there? Oh, I've been there.

CHANGING SEASONS

When I was first born again, if you brought me a bottle of Jack Daniels, I might have really had to fight the pressure to take a drink. You might have felt the pressure of wanting to take a drink when you first got saved. You might have been born again in your spirit, but your old body still had a lot of things going on inside that it still liked.

You could walk by a bottle of Jack Daniels, even though you were trying not to look, your eyeballs would be still trying to stretch around the back of your head, trying to see that bottle of Jack Daniels. Well, now I can walk by a bottle of Jack Daniels all day long, and never give a thought to it; I don't even know that it's there.

Why? Because it's a new season. The season has changed. It will be this way all your life. As long as you live in God's Kingdom the seasons will change. The reason the Devil can't defeat most of us in our old stuff is he isn't trying the old stuff anymore. He is smart enough to know attacking us in areas where we've already had victory is foolish. He looks for new areas, new seasons, new temptations.

You can be in the middle of temptation with strife, and not realize it is formulated by the Devil to cause you trouble. If you don't know what you're experiencing, you will fall into the trial. It is much easier to resist the temptation than it is to fall into the trial. Remember, the trial is never something put on you, it is something you fall into, according to James.

"Well, Brother Tim, how do you fall into the trial?" you ask. Good question! The way you fall into it is like this. The Devil opens the door with some temptation, and then, if you won't close that door, he comes right on in and brings every other evil work he can get in with him. He might come in through strife, but along with strife he brings sickness.

"How did he get that door open?" you ask. I resisted every flu commercial I've ever seen. When I'm at family gatherings and they say, "Well, we all might get sick," I stand up and say, "I don't get sick! The Word says I am healed."

Guess what? While you were slamming the door of sickness in his face and bloodying his nose with brass knuckles, he was sneaking around looking for side doors you haven't locked.

The Devil is looking for a door to get in, and if you're not careful, he will get a door open you don't think is important, or one you are sure is too small for him. (Just so you know, there is no door too small.) But once the door is open, he brings other things in with him, other than just the strife. The strife is just to get the door open. Why did I pick strife in this example? Because according to James, *"For where envying and strife is, there is confusion, and every evil work"* (3:16). Strife is one of Satan's favorite target areas. He's had a lot of success with it over the centuries.

ENTERING YOUR PROMISED LAND

Before God sends you into your promised land there are certain doors you have to learn to close first. If you don't close those doors, you might stand all day long on the promises of God. You might know every promise there is concerning healing, but you won't receive your healing until the door to the Devil is closed. What most people want is to receive the promises based on Jesus' works, but they do not want to close the door to the Devil held open by their works.

Most people just want to enter into the promised land. They don't want to change; they just want to know where the promised land is. It's like the children of Israel. They sent Moses up the mountain for some direction, saying, "We need to know, we need to hear from God, we need to know what direction to go in." Instead of coming back with directions, Moses came down the mountain with ten character issues.

Many of us have wanted the same thing from God. What we wanted is to know how we get from here to my promised land, or in some cases, my promised man. But it's like I said to one lady, "You've run the first three husbands off, why would God want to send you another one?"

What God will work on is what causes you to change on the inside. The Israelites needed to make some changes before they got into the promised land.

"But," you might protest, "isn't that receiving from Jesus based on my works?" Not at all. Our receiving is based solely on the basis of what Jesus has done for us. It couldn't be based on our works because if it was, then we would have a right to the glory. No one receives any glory but Jesus.

In Galatians 6:7 we find that God will not be mocked; whatever a man sows, he will reap. If you sow to the flesh corruption, then He says you will reap corruption. Not only must I stand on the promises of God so I don't sow corruption with my words, I must learn to close the door to the devil so I don't sow corruption with my works.

Now, a better way of stating this is in Joshua 1:8 says, **"...but thou shalt meditate therein day and night, ...for then thou shalt make thy way prosperous."** If God gave you five million dollars, and you didn't have the wisdom to get that five million dollars in the first place, you would lose it. If you don't have the wisdom to receive it, you don't have the wisdom to keep it.

If Jesus gave most pastors 10,000 people, they would run it down to about 250, because that's about all the vision they have inside of them, because the 10,000 would drive them nuts.

You take Donald Trump, for instance. That guy thrives on getting into a situation that *has* to work, or he knows he's going to fail. He's turning his deals over here and over there and he thrives on the bigness of his vision. Ministers who are being successful in God at 10,000, thrive off large numbers. But you take someone who hasn't changed inside, he doesn't have the wisdom or the vision, and he'll just lose the whole deal or whittle the 10,000 people down to 250, because that's what he has on the inside of him.

Even if Jesus gave you a business, and you didn't have the wisdom to make the business work, you would lose the business. What Jesus will begin to work on is what's keeping you from having the success inside of you, because before you have success out there, you first of all must have success inside.

So what Jesus will do is come to you and say, "Listen, you need to make some changes inside—in your heart." The problem with us making changes inside us is that usually we don't know they need to be made. The changes need to be made *before* we go into the promised land. Then God got personal with me.

THE LIST

It came about during a time when I had gotten alone with God to spend time seeking Him. I had been listening to Louise Brock's teaching tapes on *The Anointing to Spoil*, when He presented me with a list of character issues.

Now I usually don't talk about the list. You know, there are things on that list that shocked me. Things like not being faithful, stealing, and lying. Of course, I couldn't believe it was for me because I couldn't see how those things applied to me. I said, "That list is not for me, I can tell you right now, that list doesn't belong to me. There are things on that list that I know that I don't do, and it's no part of me, it has nothing to do with me, that list can't belong to me!"

Do you know what Jesus said? Nothing. He's not the one having trouble. He's not the one stuck in the mud. He's not the one stuck out there in the desert.

Then I tried to make everybody else own up to that list because there were things on it I wasn't willing to admit were for me. I tried to make it fit everybody else. I'd be doing some pastoral counseling, and I'd wait until we got real deep into it, until they cried, and almost wanted to beat each other. Then I would unscroll the list and say, "Is this you? You know what God thinks about lying? You know your marriage would work if you'd own up to the list."

I even had some friends call me, and right in the middle of our conversation, I'd say, "Has the Lord been dealing with you about a list?"

"Well, not particularly."

"Well, maybe I put it the wrong way. Are there some changes you need to make?" Everybody in the ministry is always saying, "I need change, I need change." But none of them would own up to that list.

Finally, the Lord began to reveal to me that the list was mine! He started at the top of the list with faithfulness. Faithfulness was at the very top of the list.

As I began to work on some of this list, the Lord pointed to some things on there He said were for me. And, again, I couldn't believe it was for me, because the problem with being blinded with these problems, is exactly that, you don't know you have them. For example, I've seen some people so rude that they thought they were funny, but they were rude. They said, "Well, that's the way my mama was, that's the way that I am, it's just my personality." Of course, they're the last to know how rude they are. They illustrate the problem with being deceived, (if you are deceived you never know you are) by not recognizing their abrasive attitude. So the problems that hold you back are usually a form of deception.

THE FIRST ISSUE

In Matthew 25, Jesus talks about the talents.

For the kingdom of heaven is as a man traveling into a far country, who called his own servants, and delivered unto them his goods. And unto one he gave five talents, to another two, and to another one; (Matt. 25:14-15)

But the most important principle is in verse 21. It says,

His lord said unto him, Well done, thou good and faithful servant: thou hast been faithful over a few things, I will make thee ruler over many things:...

See, you will think that the little things don't matter, but God will assign little things before He assigns big things. The first issue is faithfulness.

He wanted me to make the change on the inside of me, because I was the one having the trouble. I said, "Well, where do I learn about faithfulness?" The Lord said, "I want you to study the men of old."

I thought about it for a few moments, and I don't know why I said this, but I said, "Are you talking about Brother Oral?" thinking He was talking about Oral Roberts. I admire Brother Oral Roberts. Anybody who's seen millions of people saved, built a City of Faith when everybody was fighting and calling him a bunch of rotten names, and still accomplished the work of God, has to be a faithful man.

THE GUY WITH THE BOAT

The Lord said, "No, I want you to start with Noah."

I thought about Noah. "Noah? You mean the boat guy, Noah? What's a guy with a boat going to teach me?" At this point I was just arguing with God. "I mean, when's the last time you read any great sermons on Noah?" I complained.

Fact is, from my Southern Baptist days, while we preached on Noah it wasn't because of his faithfulness. We were good at getting you to rededicate every Sunday. We were trained in Charles Finney. He believed a good preacher would find a sin. Then when you found a sin, start talking about the sin until you see guilt. When you start to see guilt, then bring them up and get them "across the line" to rededicate.

Every Sunday, if you were already saved, it was our job somehow or other to get you to feel guilty. We thought we were preaching and calling down conviction but basically it ended up just being guilt. But we had to get you across that line, because if you wanted to go back and preach at that church again, your preaching ability depended upon how many folks you could get down to the altar. They thought if you couldn't get anybody down front, you didn't have any ability.

As good Southern Baptists, we knew we had to get you to rededicate every Sunday, and that's where Noah came in. Sometimes we would preach sermons about Noah's boat lifting off and if you waited too long to make the decision to receive Jesus as your Lord and Savior, you'd miss the boat. Now it's in the middle of the storm and the ark's lifting up. If our preaching was going good, we could hear you start to scratch on the boat, and we knew we were getting somewhere. We'd have you believing, by the time you got home tonight, you were going to be run over by a Mac truck. Then we'd hear you scratching and hollering, "I want in, I want in." I'd say, "It's too late, you've waited too long. The doors are closed, the rain's coming, and this boat's leaving."

I told God, "That's the only sermon I know about Noah." I mean, I could get you to rededicate, but then after you rededicate, what do you do?

Now if Noah is going to be one of the keys to success in ministry, I'm concerned because I've never gone to a seminar and heard, "Today's sermon will be based upon the successful ministry of Noah. If you run your ministry and follow after him, you will have the same success. Now, let's study brother Noah." I've never heard that before.

I said, "What in the world is a man with a boat going to teach me?"

Immediately Jesus spoke up inside and said, "Every boat I've assigned to you, you let sink before you got it to the other side." I realized at least the disciples had sense enough to ask Jesus for His help. I knew I had work to do.

CHAPTER 2
AN UNSINKABLE SHIP

I said, "Well then, let's go study Noah for awhile." As I began to study about Noah, the Holy Ghost spoke to me, and I began to realize something. Imagine this: Noah comes home one day saying, "Sweetheart, honey drops." Now Mrs. Noah knows something's coming, she's seen that look before. He doesn't just say, "Oh, I want to tell you something." He's got to pave the way with words that reach in and stroke her emotions. So he says, "Oh, you're the most beautiful thing I think I've ever seen in my whole life. Have I ever told you how much I appreciate you? I even love your mama." By now she knows something is up, he's stroking too hard.

Noah says, "I've heard from the Lord." And she's heard that before! I mean, my wife has heard that from me a number of times. Mrs. Noah says, in her most patient tone, "You have?" The problem is, when you're having a lot of problems, it's amazing how much you hear from Him...and none of it is Him. Every time something pops up, you say, "That's Jesus, I've seen Him, He wants me to do it." You don't care if you're called to do it or not, you just want to do it, because you feel like it. Besides, who knows, it might get you out of the problem you're in.

Now Noah says, "I have heard from the Lord."

She says, "Well, what did you hear?"

"Well, we're going to build a boat."

Now Noah's ready to build a boat, but he's never seen a boat. He lives in a desert. He's never even been around water. He can't say, "Oh, look. There goes one. I like that kind of boat over there, I think that's the kind of boat we need to build. Look at that boat, honey, that's the one I want." There had never been a boat before. So she says the only logical thing she can say...

"WHAT'S A BOAT?"

"It's a thing that floats, and listen to this. Let me tell you what else the Lord has shown me." Have you ever seen anybody who has seen something from the Lord? You can't control them. They're like three Amway salesmen wrapped up together, or like some guy who just won the 25 million dollar jackpot. They're squirrely. They're trying to be normal, they'll sip coffee with you a little bit, and then, out of nowhere, they say, "Have I shown you this?" They start drawing things on a napkin, and then they realize it's a wrong time, like during dinner. When they see the look on your face they say, "Well, we'll talk about that a little later," and they fold up their scribbling and stick it in their pocket and try to be normal. It's all they can do to wait until they can get that napkin back out to show you the vision God has given them.

Then Noah says, "Sweetheart, it's going to be this big," and he runs down about 625 feet. When he comes back he says, "And we're going to put the tigers in the front of the boat. We're going to build a special compartment for the tigers because you know their temperament. They can't get along with anybody, so we're going to put them in the front of the boat. Stay with me, honey, I've seen the vision."

Pacing and waving his arms, he continues, "Now for balance purposes, we're going to put the elephants, because there are going to be two of them, one on the left and one on the right." He points to both sides. "They're going to balance the boat. Listen to this, I'm going to put the cobras back over here in a little special compartment, because you know how they are... ."

By this time you can imagine Mrs. Noah is looking kind of bewildered. She's trying her best to see what her husband sees.

"I've never seen an ocean, Noah."

"I know, sweetheart. But we're going to build a boat in the desert! Isn't that great? Then God is going to make it rain." And she's looking like, "Oh, sure."

MRS. NOAH

You know, women never do anything just to be doing it. Women always have a purpose in everything they do. So she's thinking, "Noah, honey, you know I've been through Amway with you and we did those condos in Denver." She knows this is not going to be as easy as it sounds, but he's fully persuaded he must be faithful to do what God has told him.

Remember, it took Noah 100 years to build the boat, and he used a pitch-like substance that was so unbelievably sticky to put the boat together and to seal it so it wouldn't leak. So you know some days Noah got pitch on his hands, and you know there had to be some days that he reached up to think about something, and his hands stuck to his head.

Noah walks through the front door and Mrs. Noah says, "Kids, go get the neighbor next door, Dad's hands are stuck to his head again. Noah, I told you to keep your hands away from your face!"

He built for 100 years and received no personal gain at all, no money, no emotional gratification, no position. Nobody appreciated Noah. All he did was take his family out there and work the daylights out of them. I mean, I could imagine his kids saying, "Oh Dad, if we didn't love you so much, we wouldn't be doing this."

He'd say, "Oh son, you've got to listen. We've got to build that compartment, we've got to get food for the elephants, we've got to get this done. You know it's going to rain any day." Because the man who has vision is in a hurry. I can recognize somebody who doesn't have any vision, they're just moving in slow speed. But if you have vision, it's, "Get out of my way. Have I shown you the new addition?" You see their hand reach for that napkin and you think, "No, please, I thought I was going to get out of here. I'm going to be stuck here for another 35 minutes listening to your ideas for the senior's ministry." You want them to stop, but they can't. They're fully persuaded. In the telling of the vision, they are being faithful to it.

What God has called you to do is be faithful in some area. No personal gratification, just faithfulness.

FAITHFULNESS

Most people in church, if you don't give them some gratification or acceptance, they're not going to do very much. But what I'm talking about is faithfulness unto God, and as you are faithful unto God, then God will reward you. In fact, what the Lord told me was, "Everything you do in the ministry will be a credit to Noah's account. Noah was faithful for 100 years, and because of his faithfulness, you are here. If he wasn't faithful, you wouldn't be here. So everything you do is accounted to Noah's account." He said, "Noah is receiving much off of what everyone else does."

Church is some place you are called to attend; it isn't something you choose. You think, *"Listen, Brother Tim, I was letting my fingers do the walking in the phone directory, and I chose the church myself."* No, you had the Angel Gabriel helping you. You wanted to go to the First Church of the refrigerator and you got sent to the church you attend. You tried your best to make it to the First Church, and circumstances—named Gabriel—kept setting you up. Jesus will not only call you to attend, but He will call you to be faithful because He values faithfulness.

HEARING HIS VOICE

The Lord gave us a building for our ministry in 1997. It was an expensive building and it's paid for. Well, in the month of June that year, the Lord told me to take about six weeks off; all of June and part of July. I was concerned about our income; we had no meetings for all that time, but I was obedient. The result was I saw more money than I had in ten years. It came from different sources. See, also on that list I told you about was money. I knew that God doesn't mind you having the money, He just doesn't want the money to have you. Luke 16:10 says that if you're unfaithful in the unrighteous mammon, He won't use you in the true riches, so you have to prove yourself faithful in the money area.

In the month of June, here comes these large sums of finances. It started one day when I was praying. I have found out I need to set time aside, to make contact with Jesus everyday. It might take ten minutes, it might take a half an hour, it might take three hours. However long it takes, I'm going to make contact with Jesus. Sometimes I just wake up, and I've already made contact. I need to make contact, not just knowing *about* Him, but knowing Him.

While I was in prayer in July, I heard my wife talking on the phone from the other room. I never listen to what the conversation is, because I usually know it's somebody wanting something. But I heard my wife say, "I don't think we're interested in that."

On the inside of me, the Holy Ghost jumped up and I ran into the room where Donna was and said, "We're not interested in what?" She said, "Well, they want us to look at this building."

I said, "Tell them we'll go look at it."

Usually I take things really slow, especially when it involves large sums of money, and more especially when I'm the guy paying for it. I mean, if they're going to give it to me, it doesn't take me long. "Yeah, you heard from Jesus. That's right, go ahead, I know it's God."

But if it's my money, I say, "Let me think about this for a little while, I've got to pray about it." Then I put my hands behind my back so no one can grab my hand and make any agreements and I think about it a little bit.

Well, I walked inside the building, and Jesus said, "Tell them you'll take it." I said, "We'll take it." I didn't even look through it, I just walked inside, took a few steps and within 20 seconds, I said, "We'll take it." Then, all of a sudden, the pressure hit my mind, *"You'll take it? Are you stupid?"* I mean, the Devil really knows how to crank up pressure when you step out of that boat. "Haven't you looked, it's storming out here? You know, you don't have any money, you just told them you'd buy the building. You want to close escrow as soon as possible and you think you'll have the money at the end of closing. What are you, nuts?"

Now if my great aunt had died, and she had left me lots of money, I would have understood. I would have said that was Jesus, and I appreciated that He set it up. But all the money we got that July came from very different sources. Even the owners donated a large portion of the building. We bought the building...and paid for it in nine days.

HOW DID YOU DO THAT?

"Jesus," I said, "I don't want to sound like I'm in unbelief here, you know I'm a man of faith. You know I don't want to get in trouble with you, but, ah, I'd like to know what I've done to get those big sums, because I might want to do it again. Just in case you're going to call me to do something else, I'd like to know why those big sums of money came in."

The Lord spoke to me out of 1 Peter 3:7 about how your prayers are hindered when there is an indifference or disagreement. I had some people working for me who were not in agreement with the vision the Lord had given us. I had to release some individuals. After they were gone we had harmony again. Our faith was no longer hindered. That's when the money started coming in.

Now, I learned a long time ago that, for my wife and me, when it came time to believing God, the more mature person has to yield, to surrender and serve the weaker person. Maturity doesn't try to make everybody get in line. Maturity has the ability to work with your family, or work with your wife.

My wife is a lot smarter than I am. Some of you have figured that out about your wives as well. There's a rational management ability that God saw we men were weak in, so He gave it to them. I'm not saying we're not intelligent men, but we don't like details sometimes. Women like details. God saw what we were lacking and supplied it in our wives.

It's important to God how we handle our family, how we deal with our wife, how we deal with our children. He takes a look at that to see how faithful we are in those areas. See, once you're married, God expects you to take care of your wife. In 1 Cor. 7:7-9 Paul made reference to the fact that some people are gifted from God with the ability to remain single. But I'm not one of those gifted ones; I've got to have my wife.

Most of us are not gifted in remaining single. We're just like Adam was. God looked down one day and said, "You know, it's not good for that boy to be by himself. That boy needs help."

I found out with my wife we have to agree together to stay in harmony so our prayers are not hindered. Sometimes she doesn't have the full vision, because I'm the one hearing from God. I'm way out in the vision. I'm saying, "Man we're going to build a big boat," and she reels me back in. It ends up being a smaller boat, but we can agree on it. We're better off agreeing on the smaller boat than we are trying to have a big boat in strife, because as long as we have disharmony, according to 1 Peter 3:7, our faith will be hindered. That's why I had to release some of those individuals working in our ministry.

So to keep my faith from being hindered out on the road my wife and I work together, we come into agreement. I've learned to submit to her in some areas. Then I don't put pressure on her, because I want to find out where she's coming from. The last thing I want to do is make her feel guilty because she doesn't want to do a big boat. Then she would have no faith. What I do is, I find out where she's at; we build the boat on that, and God makes the boat grow. When you have agreement, you have growth; no agreement, no growth. I don't care if the boat is really small, but I'm telling you there will be two happy people in the boat. That's faithfulness to my wife and our covenant.

IT'S NOT "I"...IT'S "US"

Now when I got married, the first thing I learned was it wasn't "I" anymore, it was "US." I had to check with US all the time; what is US going to do today? Is US going to go see mama today, or is US going to go camping this weekend? What does US want to do? Some of you have been married a couple of times, and you don't like that US part, you would like to be married but not have the US part in there. That's not the deal, marriage is US.

Jesus looks to see how you handle US, and if you don't handle US very well, He isn't about to turn His family over to you. He looks to see how you handle your children before He gives you charge over His. When my daughter got to be about the age of 14, she tried to be just as ungodly as she possibly could be. Here I am, a man of God, preaching and praying. She had been taught the Word of God, and then BAM, just like that she jumps up and gets rebellious.

Before then we all marched around because I was highly disciplined. We all looked like we had our ducks in a row. Here comes my family: they're all dressed alike, they all look alike, they all talk alike, they're all polite.

My children came to church and they didn't misbehave on the front row, they didn't do anything they weren't supposed to do. If they did, I'd look at them, and say, "One, two, three," and I would wait until the next day to discipline them. Now that's strong believing in discipline. That brings a change, and shows you're not just acting to the moment. They knew when dad said you'd had it, you'd had it!

Well, because of my daughter's age I couldn't whip her. She was getting to be just like her mama, she knew how to say no. I said, "God, it's that woman you gave me that's causing her to be this way." I really didn't know what to do. Nothing seemed to be bringing our daughter back into family harmony.

IT'S YOUR FAULT

Jesus woke me up in the middle of the night. I don't know if He sent Gabriel down to shake the dog snot out of me or what, but I woke up in the middle of the night. Jesus spoke out loud and said, "It's your fault." I knew what He was talking about because I had gone to bed thinking about it. "It's your fault she's the way she is; you're not taking an interest in her."

I said, "Jesus, what do I do?"

He said, "Start believing now for a husband for her. Start to trust Me for a good husband for her now." Then one day I saw the one the Lord had picked for her. He said, "There's your future son-in-law." He had hair down to his waist, he came tromping around looking like he just gotten off some boat or something.

I said, "Oh no! Devil, you get behind me in the Name of Jesus."

So help me, Jesus said, "That's your future son-in-law."

I said, "Get behind me Devil, in the Name of Jesus."

I couldn't believe my daughter would drag in something that looked that undisciplined. I found out that he was raised in an orphanage, but eventually had been accepted in the armed forces, a Special Forces unit. He was more disciplined than I ever thought about being, but he had come to a point of rebellion in his life because of the extreme discipline.

What Jesus said was, "I want you to take an interest in your daughter. You're talking to her like she's a dog: sit, roll over." He said, "I hold her accountable for her actions. She can go to hell because I hold her accountable for her decisions. If I can hold her that responsible at her age, you had better start talking to her a little differently." He said, "She is old enough to choose to go to hell, so you take an interest in her."

I said, "How do I take an interest?"

He said, "Listen to her. Don't surmise something when you don't know all the facts, and then give her some little speech. Don't give her some little word of wisdom, like, 'Oh yes, I remember back when I was a child, you know, I was like that too, but this is how I overcame it'." That's what I had been doing, so she was shutting me off altogether. From her point of view Dad hasn't got a clue as to what's going on. You remember when you got smarter than your parents because they didn't care about you?

I said to Donna, "Jesus woke me up. Wake up, wake up." When God wakes me up, I wake Donna up. And she's thinking, "Oh no, not another boat." So we went in to our daughter's room and woke her up in the middle of the night. I said, "We're going to take an interest in you." And she's like, "Yeah, Dad, yeah, Dad, okay, okay, Dad."

I started by taking her out. After school we'd go talk and spend time, and I said, "You know if you talk to me, you can tell me anything, and I'll never discipline you over anything you tell me, but if I find out that you were running and trying to lie to me, then obviously I would have to be the father that I need to be. Then I would have to discipline. But if you talk to me, I won't say a word, and I won't correct you." I said, "If God tells me something, we'll try to work on it."

HORROR STORIES

She took me at my word and tested me severely. She came in and she said some things to me. I had to hang onto my seat, and I'm thinking, *"I'm going to go out and get the small children's ballbat in the garage, and I am going to beat some of the girls she runs around with, and then when I come home, I'm going to beat her mama, and when I get through beating their mama, I'm going to beat her dad."*

When she'd finished telling me her horror stories, she asked, "Now, Dad, what do you think about that?"

I shook, and couldn't think of anything to say. The best I could come up with was, "Life is tough."

She said, "Is that it?"

"I've got to go downtown, I'll be back a little later," I said. Then I would go out and run 20 miles. I wanted to clobber somebody, but I began to take an interest in her. Amazingly enough the first thing I knew, she started listening to me, and I started listening to her. She knew, as long as I didn't lecture her, we could become friends. To this day we're best friends. I'm good friends with my son, and my wife and I have a perfect, excellent relationship, due to my wife more than me. But my daughter and I have a special relationship because we talk all the time; we listen to each other. I've learned to take an interest in her.

APPLYING THE LESSON LEARNED

So when it comes to us operating on the evangelistic field, I've learned to surrender to my wife, and we work together. I can remember when it came to giving, I wanted to tithe and she didn't want to. I said, "What can we do?" She said, "I think we can do five percent." The Lord said, "Do that, do five percent. Five percent you can grow from." We got into agreement and God started to bless our finances.

There were times when I wanted to say to my wife, "Now sweetheart let me tell you, I know a better way to do this." But to keep unity, we built a smaller boat, and the smaller boat turned into a larger boat, because with unity you'll have success. In fact in Genesis 11:4-6, God says, even in carnality, if you have unity, there is nothing impossible to you. Acts 4:24-31 explains the power of unity culminating in the room being shaken and the infilling of the Holy Ghost.

God will look to see how faithful you are to your wife, if you'll love her and surrender to her. Anybody can surrender if the circumstances are right. It takes a mature person to surrender when the circumstances are adverse and there's extreme emotional pressure.

God can only use you according to how much pressure you can resist. If pressure interferes with your faithfulness then there will be limits to how much God can use you in ministry. Family life usually has a way of exposing your limits.

CHAPTER 3

HIS CHARACTER – YOUR CHARACTER

She walked into my office with a look I had come to know on my sheep. It translates into, "I'm angry at God for the way things are, but I can't be mad at Him, so I'm coming to you to find out what God is up to in my life."

Attractive, well dressed and well spoken, she had been a long time member of the flock. She wore her forty some years well and after she sat down and we exchanged pleasantries, she launched into her story.

God, it seemed, had not done His part. After all, she had been faithful in church, upright in conduct and kept up both her house and her appearance. So where was the husband she felt God had promised her? In her mind she had earned the promised husband, so...where was he? Why wasn't God doing His part?

Now, so that you don't think I was just plain cruel to the woman, you need to know that Linda, (not her real name), was a very religious person, almost legalistic. She carried a mental balance sheet around in her head all the time, and regularly made mental notes on it. That balance sheet was her final authority. It gave her the confidence to believe her evaluation of any given situation was correct. It told her what she needed to do and what should be done for her. A constant stream of judgments flowed from the results of her tallying, and as far as she was concerned, on this matter of God doing what He said He would, things just didn't add up.

All kinds of advice came to mind as I sat and listened to her self-justification. At first I was tempted to think, *"Yeah God, why haven't you sent her a husband?"* Then I thought, *"I'm glad it wasn't me,"* assuming I was single. And just as I began exploring why this woman and her balance sheet would be so hard to live with, the Lord spoke up on the inside of me and gave me the words to give her. I knew they would shock her and perhaps anger her, but He would definitely get her attention with them.

"You've run off the last three He sent you; why should He send you another one?"

Her mouth opened to challenge what I said, and then clamped shut. She tried again. Nothing would come out. Finally, she rose and mumbled a thank you for my time and left. She had some thinking to do. That balance sheet would have to go, and she would have to make room in her heart for the grace of God that would send her what she needed, not what she deserved.

ARE WE LISTENING?

Just as in Linda's case, we too need to learn that everything we receive from Jesus must be based on His works, not ours. Because it is our works, or what we do in the natural, that the Devil works on to gain entrance. Most often his attacks center on character issues. What the Holy Ghost works on is the inside of us, so we are able to stand on the promises because, again, everything we receive is based on Jesus' works.

In John 5:1-15 you will find the story of Jesus healing the man at the pool of Bethesda. This man who was crippled had laid beside this pool for 38 years.

Now 38 years is a long time to be paralyzed, not to mention the indignity of not being in control of any bodily functions. After Jesus healed him He came to him in the Temple and said, "Sin no more, least something worse come on you." Now I read this and I think, what in the world could be worse than 38 years of being totally paralyzed, with all the physical problems, self-esteem problems and family problems which would go along with all of that? What could be worse than that?

But if we are to believe Jesus, there must be something else that could be worse. The point Jesus is making to the man is not just that there is potential for something worse, but that it was sin that he let into his life years ago that got him in the condition he had been in.

Now we know that lack of faith in standing on the promises of Jesus will allow the Devil to get in and take advantage of our unbelief. But, he also takes advantage of the things inside of us where there is a breach of character.

What you will find then is, before God can send you to do a job for Him, or before He can give you your heart's desire, it is necessary for you to close the door to the Devil in your own life. If you won't, then standing on the promises of the Word will cause blessings to come to you only to be lost, or in some cases, not received at all. We stand on the promises, and get Jesus to meet our needs because Jesus has already paid the price for us to receive the blessing. It's a done deal from His end. But if the Devil owns any part of us, we will never get the fullness of what God intended us to have.

When we have the door of sin open to allow the Devil to get in and mess something up, he doesn't stop there. If the door is open to lying, he tempts us with lying and stealing. In other words, we are extending an invitation to him to bring even worse things with him.

The Devil will work on something within your character, which, unfortunately for some of us, is not hard to do.

One old boy said, "I had four chances to sin, and I turned three of them down." He was pretty proud he had turned down three of the four. But the Devil was still able to get in. We have all been down that path, where we have had an opportunity to turn down chance after chance, only to get caught in the very last one. Now the reason it is always the last one is because the Devil doesn't need any more once he's overcome you in that one. He might have had a barrel full of other temptations planned, but they were no longer needed.

Once that one sin is there, the Devil has a toe hold. Then he works it up into a foot hold, then a strong hold and finally a strangle hold. His goal is to choke the life of God out of anything you do. And he's willing to start small.

THIEF

I couldn't get away from that doggoned list. "Lord, this list can't be for me," I said, "I saw thievery on that list, thievery. Now Lord, You know You told me one time, on 2550 Altamont Drive, here in Klamath Falls, Oregon, that I would not steal. In fact You told me I wouldn't go down the street and steal something, that's what You told me. And now I see thievery on that list. You asked me why I wouldn't go down and steal, and You said to me—You didn't call me Dr. McFall or anything—You said Tim, you wouldn't go down the street here and steal something, would you?" And I said "No, I wouldn't even think of it."

He said, "You are not willing."

"That's right," I said.

"Well, there are some things in Me that you are not willing to do either," He said. "You want the anointing to minister, and that's fine, but the anointing doesn't come and then you get willing. You get willing and then the anointing comes."

To make the point clear and real to me He was showing me that because I wasn't willing to steal I never did. But if I had been willing to steal, then thievery would have come.

He said, "There are some things I want you to do, but you're not willing to say, 'Yes Lord, let it be that way'." Later on I would find out what exactly I had been stealing, but for now the Lord wanted me to understand the importance of being willing to do or not do His will. We get the whole thing backwards sometimes.

It is just like somebody who says they will be willing to go to China when they feel an overwhelming burden for the people, or feel a tremendous sense of anointing for ministry. It doesn't work like that. First of all you get willing, and then you get the anointing.

It works the same way when you are in prayer. You don't go pray and then get willing, you get willing and then comes the anointing for you to pray.

You first get willing to win souls, and then you will go soul winning. You don't go soul winning and then get willing. So, to make the point the Holy Ghost said, "You first of all must be willing to obey Me."

I thought this thief business was about money, so I mentally searched all my giving for the last while and found a few instances where I hadn't given what I felt prompted to give. In some cases I had not given at all when I felt I should have. I knew the choice was mine, but perhaps He was hanging me on a technicality here. So I confessed all the things I could find where I had come up short in the giving department, only to find out He wasn't talking about money at all. But, since I had brought up the subject of money, He wasn't going to let the opportunity pass by without taking full advantage of it.

OPPORTUNITY FOR INCREASE

What He said to me was, "I want to increase your receiving."

Well now, I don't know about you, but I was ready for some of that. If God wanted to increase the amount of money He was giving to me, I was willing to go with the money issue. I said, "Okay, if You want to increase the amount of money You're giving to me, I want to hear what You have to say. I am definitely willing on this one."

Since this had all come within the context of that list the Holy Spirit had given me, I assumed there would be some changes required of me.

He said, "I want to increase your finances, the amount that I'm using to sow back to you." I said, "Well, You know, I'm willing for that, I mean, let's get with this, I'm willing to make changes."

Then the Lord showed me a picture. He said, "Up to now you've been using an eight ounce cup to sow with, so I've been using an eight ounce cup to sow to you." He said, "I run all over, angels are running here, they're getting eight ounces here, and eight ounces there, and eight ounces way over here. We need to increase this," He continued, "I want to increase it from eight ounces to half a gallon."

THE HALF GALLON CHALLENGE

Now I had already started to see where the ministry was going to require large sums of money to finance some of the things the Lord had shown me, such as television and some other commitments we had made. But He told me sums that would make your mind stagger.

Well I don't know about you, but I'm interested in God using a half a gallon as the measure He blesses me with, and I knew the principle of sowing and reaping.

In Luke 6:38, Jesus said, *"For with the same measure that ye mete withal it shall be measured to you again."* So whatever measurement you use is what He uses. If you sow sparingly, you will reap sparingly and according to what measurement you use then, God uses that same measurement to sow back to you. The Apostle Paul confirms this principle in 2 Corinthians 9:6. *"But this I say, He which soweth sparingly shall reap also sparingly; and he which soweth bountifully shall reap also bountifully."*

So the Lord says, "Okay, I want you to increase it to half a gallon."

Now, if the Lord came to you and said, "I want to start using a half gallon measurement to sow back to you," would you be interested in that?

Well, I was definitely interested in that. I wanted those half gallon size blessings. So I asked, "How do we do this?"

He said, "I want you first to be willing to sow a half gallon to Me. Just have the willingness to say 'Yes Lord, I am willing to sow a half gallon'."

He said, "I want you to make a commitment from within; the willingness is there, just say, 'Yes Lord, I will sow a half gallon, I make a commitment to do it'. If you are willing to sow that, then I will provide seed for you to sow. Did I not say that I would minister seed for the sower?" 2nd Corinthians 9:10, *"Now he that ministereth seed to the sower both minister bread for your food, and multiply your seed sown, and increase the fruits of your righteousness;"* declares the same truth.

THE WILLINGNESS KEY

My willingness was the key. Willingness is the key to both a blessing and sin. Just like David's willingness to say yes to Bathsheba led to sin (2 Samuel 11:2-4), I had the willingness to sow money as seed and it led to a blessing.

See, we sin first from within with our willingness to sin. David looked over his banister and saw Bathsheba bathing on a nearby rooftop and said, "Uh-huh," the expression of his willingness to sin. We thought a commercial came up with that, "Uh-huh" stuff. No, it started with David, that "Uh-huh" business has been around for a long time. All it takes to sin is to say, "Uh-huh."

And when the sin conceives inside, it eventually brings forth death: *"Then when lust hath conceived, it bringeth forth sin: and sin, when it is finished, bringeth forth death."* according to James 1:15.

Not only is sin conceived like that, by taking the thought but, praise the Lord, so is the Word. Think about Mary, the mother of Jesus. The angel appears to her and tells her she will bear the Messiah and it will be a virgin birth. Two fantastic statements. But look at Mary's response. *"Be it unto me according to thy word."* (Luke 1:38). She took the thought into her heart. She did an "Uh-huh." She received it and it became the very life of God within her.

Now, God knew I didn't have half gallons to sow with so He said, "I'll provide the seed for you to sow with, if you have the willingness to sow it." I said, "Okay Lord, I'll sow the half gallon. I make that commitment before You; the half gallon is Yours, I'll sow the half gallon."

But then, you know what I did? When I had the money instead of sowing the half gallon, I only sowed the tithe on it. That's called stealing. I chose not to recognize what God had sent me as seed, but rather as increase. I tithed on my seed instead of giving it. Big difference! And worse yet, I realized my harvest would be proportionately smaller as well.

When I realized what I had done I felt really bad. I figured this is what God had been talking about when He put thievery on that list He gave me. God had caught me. He had caught me on a point I recognized. In a way I felt like He had hung me on a technicality. But the Lord said, "No, that's not it."

"That's not it?" I said, "You mean I'm down here on the floor fessing up to this, and that's not even the point You were trying to make?"

He said, "No, no, I knew you'd get that one eventually and it would get hold of you. I knew your heart was right; that wasn't what I was referring to."

"Well then, where is the thievery?"

He said, "I want you to read Acts the 12th chapter."

"Acts the 12th chapter?" I asked. I'm thinking, *"Thievery in Acts the 12th chapter? What kind of thievery verses are in there?"*

The first 19 verses of the chapter tell of Herod the King killing

James the brother of John, and of Peter's escape from jail. The next four verses tell about Herod's death when he gave a speech before a foreign delegation, and the last two verses talk about the Word of God multiplying, and the return of Barnabas and Saul from Jerusalem.

"What thievery?" I wondered.

And then I got to thinking about it. Here was Herod killing several members of the early Church just to please some political allies, and he goes so far as to kill one of the foundational apostles, James.

Now, James, along with John and Peter, formed the inner circle of Jesus' staff. James and John were the Zebedee brothers, the Sons of Thunder. These were the boys who wanted to call down fire on a village after the people had rejected Jesus. They wanted to sit on the right and left hand sides of Jesus in His kingdom. Jesus answered that request by saying it wasn't His choice. He almost sounds like if it had been up to Him they might have gotten their wish. So evidently Jesus loved James.

So King Herod, having already killed a number of believers, now kills James with a sword. The shocker is, God doesn't do anything about it. We find out in verse 23 that He strikes Herod dead. But it wasn't for the murder of James!

Herod is struck down because he attempted to steal God's glory! Thievery!

Very quietly then, Jesus said to me, "Now, I use you in anointings, and miracles, and healings, but at times you've been stealing My glory."

Oh! Oh! Oh! I wanted to find a hole and hide...quick.

CHAPTER 4
STEALING IS STEALING

I was in Bend, Oregon, one night enjoying the worship service and getting ready to minister when the Lord called my attention to this little old lady standing next to me.

As I started to step to the front to take the service, I saw her in the Spirit reach up into a cupboard, and take out something in a bottle. She poured it in a whiskey jigger, set the bottle down, put the cap on it, and put it back up into the cupboard. Then I saw her take the drink. When she did, she shook her head back and forth several times and made a terrible face like it was the worst tasting whiskey she had ever had. She set the jigger back down on the counter, and the vision ended.

By now I'm up on the platform just standing there seeing this whole scene in the Spirit and thinking how silly I must look just standing there and doing nothing. Then of course I begin to consider what the Lord wanted me to do with this. I figured He wanted me to rebuke her. *"That must be what He wants,* I thought; *she's a hypocrite. She's standing up in church acting all spiritual and at home she's drinking."*

Now we know God works in special ways with baby believers; He nurtures babies. But hypocrites, boy I'm telling you, He can be hard on those folks. Someone who looks like they have it all together, they come to church, they act like they're perfect, they even minister, and then they run out and sin. God has a tendency to reveal that on them, just to help them and the rest of the folks to know they can't do that and get away with it forever.

So I'm thinking Jesus wants me to rebuke her. So I try out a few rebukes in my mind. I say, *"Sister, I saw you take a drink and shudder."* Then I thought, no, that's not tough enough. So I tried, *"Jesus showed you to me, and we saw you taking a drink of this stuff, and you shuddered after you drank it."* Again, not tough enough. So on the third time, in my mind I said, *"Sister, I saw you taking something out of the cupboard, you poured it into a whiskey jigger, and when you took a drink of that stuff you shuddered and made a terrible face."* Now, I felt like that one had some punch in it. So I repeated it to her.

Her response taught me a lesson I'll never forget.

"Ohhhhh," she says, "oh, that cod liver oil, it's just tastes so horrible I can hardly stand it." And she shuddered just like I saw her do in the vision. She said, "That cod liver oil, I take it for my arthritis; I have arthritis so bad and nobody knows how bad it is, and that cod liver oil seems to help with the pain."

I thought Jesus wanted to rebuke her, but what He really wanted was to let her know He understood her condition. His revealing her situation was enough to knock the arthritis right out of her body. In spite of my delivery, she recognized Jesus understood she had arthritis and He wasn't holding back her healing. She was able to then move into a position to receive her healing. And she did.

AREN'T I SOMETHING

Well instantly I thought, *"Boy, aren't I spiritual?"* Then, right behind that thought came, *"And you were going to rebuke her. Boy do I feel stupid."* Then I had to admit to myself I knew what had gone on here. I had drawn attention to myself instead of drawing attention to Jesus. Once I had understood that, the Lord spoke up on the inside of me, "If you draw attention to yourself," He said, "then you're stealing My glory, and thievery is thievery."

How many times have we taken the credit that rightfully belonged to God? "Well, I prayed for sister so-and-so and she was healed." Or, when something happens we've been praying about, we say, "You know, I prayed for that to happen." What we are really saying is, "It was my prayers that made it happen." We're stealing God's glory.

The Lord told me, "If you draw attention to yourself, it's stealing." You notice that even though John the Baptist was killed, and James the Apostle was killed, I didn't send the angel down to strike Herod dead? But the very moment he was willing to take My glory, I sent the angel (Acts 12)." He said, "You notice the angel was from Me in this case, but it could have been from the Devil because stealing is stealing."

"You quit taking the credit and glory for what belongs to Me, because that form of stealing will open the door to the Devil," He said.

If the Devil steals, he will take more than you did. When you make the decision, or the commitment to take something that doesn't belong to you, it opens the door for the Devil to steal from you. In fact, Jesus told me, "Now if you continue to steal on that level, he will use that opening to steal your life. Now you quit taking My glory!"

Needless to say, I quit that very moment.

CHAPTER 5
DECEPTION

We lie for three different reasons:

FOR PERSONAL GAIN

One Christmas, my mother and father-in-law went to buy a dog. They had previously owned a St. Bernard so they were looking for a couple of small indoor dogs. When they got to the pet store, they told the salesperson they were only interested in small breed dogs. They left the store with two puppies which the salesman assured them were small breed dogs. One of them actually was, but the other just kept on growing. So much for truth in advertising.

You find this lack of ethics in sales sometimes. The temptation to say anything to get the sale is almost irresistible to some salespeople. Some people will tell you whatever you want to hear. "It's only got 30,000 miles on it," (meaning the odometer) is what we're told, but the odometer has been turned back twice. Yes, it's a fact that it only says 30,000 miles, and they'll let you believe that is the truth, when the truth is the car itself has 90,000 miles on it. They're lying for personal gain.

FOR SELF GRATIFICATION

Then there is lying for self-gratification, or to raise a person's self-esteem. I've seen people who were so good at lying they end up believing it themselves. It doesn't matter what story you tell, they'll come up with a better one.

My brother-in-law was so proficient at lying like that, even if you knew it was a lie you would sit there and enjoy it anyway. But you couldn't contradict it, and you sure couldn't outdo him.

When a bunch of us guys got together, we'd start out telling hunting stories, but by the time my brother-in-law got done, you might as well just quit, because there was no topping him.

So we would change the topic to combat. I told them about how, before I was saved, I had been shot at by three different individuals at point blank range, and all of them missed. I'm very thankful to be alive today. I was shot at in my own house one time. We had a gun battle going on between one neighbor and another neighbor, and our house was occasionally caught in the crossfire.

Then I told them about when I was driving down the freeway, and I saw two men shoot into another car right next to me with a 12 gauge shotgun. Let me tell you, I jumped out right in the middle of the freeway, and tried to get away. I didn't want to be next. They saw me, threatened to kill me, and when I ran, they chased me down the freeway for awhile.

Now these are true stories, mind you, but I'm not telling them very dramatically. My brother-in-law immediately kicks in with a story about how he was in hand-to-hand mortal combat with a screw driver, and how many people he fended off with it. By the time he was done everybody was rolling on the floor. You would have thought he was Kung Fu man with a screw driver. I forget how many he said he wounded, but it was a lot.

Personal gratification is when you lie to gain attention.

Then we started talking about our cars breaking down. He said, "One time my car wouldn't start, and it really lined the traffic up." The way he told it, you would have thought it happened in front of the White House, but actually it was in Four Corners, Virginia. "The cars were lined up for miles," he said. "I kept trying to start it, and they kept blowing the horns," he said, "I finally jumped out of the car, and went up to the guy behind me, because he wouldn't let up on the horn. I yelled out to him, 'Hey buddy, let *me* hold the horn and let's see if *you* can get it started!'"

By the time he got through telling stories, you might as well give up. When he was done, even I believed it, he told it so well. That kind of deception is very powerful, and so real you'll be deceived by it, even though you know it's a lie. Every time you start to grab hold of them with the truth, they're able to lie again and slip out of your grip.

Some people who are so good at this, when they smell the truth getting close to them, they lie three other ways and you look like the bad guy. So after awhile you don't even want to mess with a guy like that because, if you do, you end up looking bad and they end up looking good.

Usually those who lie for self gratification do so because they have a very low self image. Usually, this begins early in their childhood. School is the training ground for learning how to lie. When they come home with a "B" on their report card, their parents tell them, "You didn't get an 'A' because you just didn't try hard enough. You could have done better."

In a child's mind, this is a form of rejection, not acceptance. And if you don't accept your children, somebody else will. If they don't feel accepted, sometimes they will start a lie to make them look better so you will accept them.

* * *

If you're married to somebody who has a very low self image, Lord help you. Because they're the type, if you say "Your hair looks good," they say, "What's the matter with my hair? You think something is wrong with my hair, or you wouldn't have told me my hair looks good. Now I want to know what's the matter with my hair?"

"No, your hair looks really good!" you say.

"No, you wouldn't have told me my hair looked good unless there was something the matter with my hair. What's the matter with my hair?"

So, finally you just say, "Oh brother, okay, okay! Just have a good day!"

"Why wouldn't I have a good day? Do you think I can't appreciate a nice day? What's wrong with me, that you think I won't have a good day?"

Then in an attempt to be nice you say, "You know, you have a good personality."

"Oh no you don't. You think I have a horrible personality. You wouldn't have brought it up, if you didn't think I had a bad attitude, or a bad personality."

Someone like that can't even receive correction. In fact, because they hear things you didn't say, it's dangerous even to talk with them most of the time. You say one thing, they hear something different. By the time it's all over, you've called them every name in the book, according to them, and you're thinking, *"Listen, all I said was 'Have a good day'!"*

These type of people give you a no-win situation, and in so doing maintain a type of control over the situation that gratifies them. It's weird, I know.

TO DEFEND THEMSELVES

Others will lie to defend themselves. This most commonly happens when people operate in fear. They don't have any hope of things getting better in their lives; their goal is maintaining the status quo, surviving. To them protection of their stuff, their self-image, or their opinion is paramount. They are nearly paranoid about being corrected or having their statements challenged.

They may not always be right but, bless God, they are never wrong.

A friend of mine has a brother-in-law like that. No matter what you might offer as an option, if Fred (not his real name) didn't think of it first it isn't any good. One day my friend was helping Fred tow his car after it had quit on him. We won't go into why it quit; that's another story. My friend did as Fred requested him to do.

Suddenly the tow rope broke and Fred lashed out, "I thought you said you knew how to do this."

In fact, my friend had never offered a single word of comment.

"You told me you knew what you were doing," Fred persisted.

Nothing my friend said could stem the tide of anger boiling out of Fred. Finally, without a word he tossed the rope to Fred and walked off. Later, in telling it at home, my friend was made out to be at fault by the lies told against him.

Children learn this technique early as a way to avoid getting into trouble with their parents. Because it works so well with their siblings and playmates, they are often amazed when their parents see through their deceptions. Parents must not let their sweet darlings get away with this kind of deception, because in the end the child will deceive themselves.

How about it? Any deceptions in your closet? The power of coming clean of all of them will amaze you. Not only that, it slams the door in the Devil's face. Remember, you won't receive all God has promised to you until you close the door of deception to the Devil. We'll look more at that in the next chapter.

CHAPTER 6
DECEPTION – PART II

And when he cometh, he findeth it swept and garnished. Then goeth he, and taketh to him seven other spirits more wicked than himself; and they enter in, and dwell there: and the last state of that man is worse than the first.

(Luke 11:25-26)

Everything we receive from Jesus must be based on what He's done for us. But we know that our works are what let the Devil get a position from which he has authority to harass and/or render us ineffective.

While we're standing on the promises of receiving from Jesus, we must also close the door to the Devil. Now we know unbelief and lack of understanding will open that door to the Devil. So as I'm standing on the promises and receiving from Jesus, I know I must stay in faith and continue in the Word and prayer to increase my faith on His works.

If I went to Jesus and tried to say, "Jesus, I know I'm going to receive healing from You because I've been attending church for the last umpteen Sundays, I've swept the floors, I haven't missed a lick when it comes to the doors being open at church," it wouldn't get me anywhere with Him. There is something wrong about asking like that, and we know it. What I receive from the Lord must be based on what He's done for me, instead of what I've done for Him. I can't receive from Jesus based on my goodness.

But on the other hand, just as unbelief will open the door to the Devil, there are other things in our lives that will open the door to the Devil.

THE DECEPTION OF OUR WORDS

"So," you ask, "what are those other things?"

Well, one of the character flaws the Devil looks for and uses to his maximum advantage is the deception of our own words...lying. Just like you received from Jesus based on His works, the Devil gets access to you according to your works. When you yield to works of unrighteousness or temptations to compromise your integrity, such as lying it opens the door to the Devil.

It started with a character flaw. The children of Israel wanted to enter into the promised land, but God had to make some changes in their lives before they could. Many times, if God gave you what you truly wanted, when you got it, you'd just mess it up. And the Israelites would have done the same thing.

The reason is, if you don't have the wisdom to gain it, you don't have the wisdom to keep it. So what God will do is, He will start by giving you the wisdom to receive so you don't lose the real thing when it finally comes.

But, remember, while you're trying to receive, the Devil is trying his best to steal it behind your back. You're trying to beat him off, but it's your character, or your works that opened the door again. And, here's the worst part, when the Devil does come back, he brings something worse than what was there before.

THE FATHER OF LIES

In John 8:44 Satan is described as the father of all lies. Just as we give Jesus place to work in our lives when His words abide within us, it works the same with the Devil. Partaking of Satan's lies allows the Devil's words to abide in us, which opens the door to the Devil.

Now you can run him off through the redemptive rights of Jesus, and you can stand on the promises, believing that Jesus' death on the cross paid the full price for everything you need. But if you leave the back door open with lies, the Devil will still tear down what you're doing.

Jesus said to me, "Close That Door." (Hence the title of this book). On the list He gave me were some things I could not believe were for me. So, I concluded the list wasn't for me. My proof was lying was on that list and I didn't believe I lied. You know, when you have a problem, you're usually the last to know.

"Jesus, I don't lie," I said.

Do you know what Jesus said back to me?

Nothing.

I have found He's a God of very few words. When He began to create the whole universe, He only said two words. I know the King James says He said, "Let there be light," but, in the Hebrew, He only said, "Light...be," and it was. God will tell you something and, if you're not willing to listen, He won't hound you over it. He generally doesn't repeat Himself.

When God gave me the list, I was intoxicated with His presence. I'm writing down, "thievery, unfaithfulness, lying and deception...," and during the anointing it felt good. Later on, when I realized the list was for me, it didn't feel so good.

He said, "If I send you, and you have a door open, the Devil will take advantage of your sin. Whatever you do in secret will be shouted from the rooftops and, not only that, he'll bring sickness in, disease in, and poverty in. He'll come in through the back door and try to bring you down."

I thought, *"Well I can stand on the promises and keep the Devil out."*

Beloved, you can stand on the promises all day long, but according to Galatians chapter 6:7, **"God is not mocked: for whatsoever a man soweth, that shall he also reap."** If you sow corruption, you will reap corruption, unless you repent of it. Lying is corrupt speech.

Another layer of deception occurs often at this point. We might ask for forgiveness, but we usually won't repent. To *repent* is to be willing to change; to turn around and go the other way, and close the doors in your life which sin has opened to the Devil.

Many times, we won't lie for personal gain, or we won't lie for self gratification, but we *will* lie to defend ourselves.

THE BELT OF TRUTH

Ephesians chapter 6 says part of the armor of God is the belt of truth. Truth is our most powerful defense against the lies of the Devil. But sometimes, because of fear, instead of defending ourselves with the Word of God, we try to defend ourselves with lies. And that just makes things worse.

No matter why we lie, sin is sin. If we are willing to lie, then Satan, the father of lies, can use that door to get into our lives. Instead of defending ourselves with lies, it's important that we defend ourselves with the Word of God. That is what the belt of truth is for, and why it's part of the armor.

It gets to me when I hear people say, "I got up this morning and I put *all* my armor on," and they don't realize part of the armor of God is character. It's not just standing on the promises of God. It is also speaking the truth, and not being willing to lie, even to our own defense.

TWO TYPES OF TRUTH

There are two types of truth. There's the facts we know, and then there is the Truth.

What do I mean by that? Here's an example.

But the men that went up with him said, We be not able to go up against the people; for they are stronger than we. And they brought up an evil report of the land which they had searched unto the children of Israel, saying, The land, through which we have gone to search it, is a land that eateth up the inhabitants thereof; and all the people that we saw in it are men of a great stature. And there we saw the giants, the sons of Anak, which come of the giants: and we were in our own sight as grasshoppers, and so we were in their sight.

(Numbers 13:31-33)

The children of Israel sent spies into Canaan, and when they came back, all they did was report the facts as they saw them. They came back and said, "It's a fact there are giants in the land." But Joshua and Caleb spoke the Truth when they said, "We can take the land."

You don't get healed just because you quit lying and believe the facts you hear. You have to stand on what Jesus has done for you, and claim the truth of those promises for yourself.

I had a friend who was terminally ill. So I went before the Lord and said, "Lord, what do I tell him?"

He said, "I want you to go tell him, 'What the doctor said is a fact', but you look him in the eye, point your finger at him, and tell him 'But, that is not the truth,' and he'll understand."

And that's what I did. I told him, "What the doctor said to you is a fact; yes, you're terminally ill, in their eyes it's a fact. But let me tell you, it's not the *truth*. The truth is, Jesus said you were healed." He said, "I see it," and just like that, it knocked the cancer out of his body. The doctors couldn't find a single bit of cancer in his entire body after that.

God got all over the children of Israel for talking facts. In fact, He called it unbelief. There are giants, and there are circumstances in your life, but God says, **"And I will send an angel before thee;"** (Exodus 33:2). You've got to be bold enough to go into the Promised Land in spite of the giants..

There is the truth found in the Word of God, then there is the factual truth. It's important for us to not only tell the truth of the Word, and stand on the promises, but also to tell the facts right.

I asked the Lord, "Why is that important?"

"Because one lie breeds more lies. You sow deception, it breeds more lies; it becomes alive, and it goes to work on you. Once that lie goes out, you have to tell another lie; if you're willing to lie once, you will lie again," He said.

And everything those lies produce will die, because God is the Truth and the Life. Truth and Life are found only in God; apart from Him, there is only death. So, even if you do gain success by telling a lie, you're guaranteed by the Word of God, to be abased and brought down.

On the other hand if, by doing it God's way, you are lifted up, then there is nothing the world can do to your company, your business, your family, or your children that can bring them down.

The Word says that however high you go, greater still will be the fall. Now, it's not very hazardous for me to jump off of a chair, but if I get up to the ceiling and then fall, I'll get hurt pretty bad. The higher you let those lies bring you, the farther and harder your fall is going to be. Consider the lie that elevates you to be your mortal enemy, because it could be the very thing that destroys you.

"WHAT DO I DO?"

"What do I do?" I said.

The Lord said, "Tell the truth." As long as you're willing to sow deception, the Devil will bring it back on you. I don't know about you, but there have been times when I didn't have a clue that somebody was trying to destroy me, as well as my whole family. It all was because I was willing to lie.

You say, "Listen, I'm standing on the promises, 'No weapon formed against me shall prosper'." Quoting Scripture always sounds good, but you can stand on those promises all you want, but if your lies are leaving doors open to the Devil, you are fooling yourself.

Let's be clear about another point right here. There have been times in my life where it would have been much easier if I had just said nothing. Unfortunately that would have been its own form of deception.

Now in sales, as in other things, sometimes you are tempted to not tell the whole truth. We call it "having reservations," because you just know if you tell too much, they won't buy. So what you learn to do is just tell the good things. You don't come out and lie, you just don't tell the whole truth. By not telling the whole truth you lead them to a conclusion that benefits you, but isn't the conclusion they would have arrived at if they had known the whole truth. By leading them to believe something different, you're lying.

You say, "But, if I'm completely honest, I can't make it work."

Listen, if you can't make it work with God's help, you're in trouble, and if you do make it work through deception, you're going to fail untimely anyway, and be brought down.

So I made a decision: If I can't do it God's way, I don't want it. If I can't make it happen God's way, I don't want it.

You say, "I don't understand that."

SELF DECEPTION

I can tell you right now, if there is something physically wrong in your body, the Holy Ghost will tell you, if you listen. But if you sow enough deception, you couldn't perceive that it's raining outside. I've seen people so spiritually dense, because they've sown deception, that they pray, meditate, and fast, but their spiritual radar doesn't pick up anything.

So I said, "Jesus, I want that door closed."

He said, "Then, tell the facts, and tell the truth."

Now, let's take the next step here. Just because you close the door to deception doesn't mean the promise is automatically going to be fulfilled. You still must stand on the promises and what Jesus has done for you.

That's the truth.

John 16:13 says that God is *"the Spirit of Truth..."* So if you walk with God, you must be willing to deal in the truth of the Word as well as the facts of the situation, because He is the Truth.

John 17:17 says, *"Sanctify them through thy truth: thy word is truth."* And in verse 19 of the same chapter Jesus says, ***"And for their sakes I sanctify myself, that they also might be sanctified through the truth."***

So, we are cleansed through the truth, and the Word is the truth. As we stand on the promises of God, the Word, we must also then sanctify ourselves from the works of the flesh by not giving place to the Devil.

You say, "Listen, I can't do business anymore! That'll ruin my business."

If that is really true of you and your business, then most of your business has been built on deception. You'll sell much more by being truthful and trusting the Lord, rather than deceiving.

If you don't want to become spiritually dense, so that you can't tell what's happening around you, then make a decision to repent and turn around, not just ask for forgiveness.

Forgiveness is when I go to another town and I say, "Father, I'm sorry for being here," but I don't leave.

Repentance is when I say, "I'm sorry for being here," and then I go back to where I need to be.

Repentance brings you to where you need to be. If you ask for forgiveness, but still don't change, you haven't gained anything. You can ask for forgiveness all day long, but He says you also must repent.

So repent today; make a decision you're not going to cross that line again and close the door to the Devil. When your circumstances tempt you to speak less than the truth, then they won't be a temptation anymore. The pressure will still be there, but it's much easier, and better, to simply do it God's way.

CHAPTER 7
STAND, THEREFORE

When I was young we lived in real poverty. I worked every evening. I'd come home from school, do my chores, and then hire out to the neighbors to do their chores. I would haul coal, chop kindling, and feed animals for other people.

I remember one particular man with special fondness because I took care of his horses. I didn't tell him, but I would have taken care of those horses for free; I loved to ride those horses. As a kid that was my favorite chore, to go ride, feed, and take care of those horses.

Several years ago we took a trip back home to Virginia. While we were there I decided to visit this man, and he made me an offer.

"Tim," he said, "I trust you. You always took excellent care of my horses, and you were dependable. I could leave, and I knew you'd be here and the horses would be taken care of. There wasn't a question about it, even when you didn't feel good. Whatever it was, you'd do the job. Now, "I want to help you," he said.

"I'll tell you what I'm going to do, just so you can come back to Virginia. I need some people I can trust, and I'm going to make it so it won't cost you a dime. I don't even want any money in return. I'm going to make the down payment for you on 40 coal trucks. I want you to go to work for me.

"In addition, I'll guarantee the haul, so you'll know that you'll get the trucks paid off." (That's a contract to guarantee that I'd be able to haul his coal for a certain period of time.) "Then," he said, "I'll help you find the drivers, and help you build the shops, just so you and I can spend some time together."

It was an incredible offer! My family and I would be set for life. It was the offer of a lifetime and with someone I genuinely liked.

What's more, some of my friends who had gotten involved in the coal hauling business had done so well they owned helicopters now. You have to be pretty wealthy to fly a helicopter just from your house to town. What had happened was, when the price of oil jumped, coal jumped from just a few dollars to over twenty dollars a ton. Nearly everybody became wealthy over night, and some of my friends had too.

So as I'm seated there, listening to my friend talk about those coal trucks, and I said, "Well, let me think about this." I did, for about ten seconds.

I said, "You know, I've always felt led into business anyway." Then I got serious. "Still, I need to pray about it. I'll let you know." I had made my decision in that ten seconds, but I thought I'd throw in the part about needing to pray so I'd sound real spiritual.

BIG DECISION

At that time we were living in a little bitty house. The outside dimensions were about 25 feet by 25 feet. The sawmill I was working for believed in keeping you tied to them; they didn't pay you enough so you could get out, even if you wanted to, but only enough to hold you captive.

I knew when I got back home what I was going to do. I was going to pack all of us up in the middle of the night, tell my mother-in-law how much we appreciated her, and head back to Virginia.

Donna wasn't to sure about all this, however. So I said, "Well

Donna, you know those split-level houses you like? How would you like to have a tri-level house, with a swimming pool in a heart shape?" I knew that would get her attention. As I started to share what the coal trucks would provide, it didn't take long for her to come around to my way of thinking.

But the path to my financial prosperity wasn't clear yet. There were minister friends who weren't sure it was God. Of course they weren't living in a 25' X 25' house either. But they began to feel much better about the idea when I reminded them how much bigger my tithe would be. It's amazing how much better people hear from God after you mention money.

So now I'm thinking, *"Man, this is looking good."* Excitement has begun to build in me. But...I said I would pray so I felt obligated to do so. I'd make it quick because God would obviously want me to do this to provide for my family.

I went back to our house, laid down on the bed and began to pray. It wasn't long until Jesus spoke up on the inside of me.

"Tim, the Devil has offered you 40 coal trucks. He offered Me the world. Are you going to take it?"

I said, "What? What did you say?" I wanted to rebuke the Devil, but I knew who it was.

He said again, "The Devil has offered you 40 coal trucks. He offered Me the world. Are you going to take it?"

I'm telling you, that put a damper on just about everything I was fixing to do. I said, Umm... ahh... well...no." I knew it was the right answer, but my heart was in my shoes. One of the hardest things I've ever done was to make the decision to walk away from that offer. One little "no" and it was all over.

BALAAM'S CHALLENGE

Hard as it was, I made a commitment before the Lord. Naturally, the Devil came immediately to challenge it.

Usually, we think the Devil just comes to speak to you. That's true, but he also comes to offer things. When someone has made a commitment to Jesus, the Devil will offer them almost anything to see if it can be used to get hold of them and, like Balaam, you will lose control.

You see, Balaam was offered a place of honor and fabulous wealth if he would go against the will of God and curse Israel. After several conversations with God, men and even his donkey, he nearly gave in to the temptation. Only after it nearly cost him his life, and God had made his donkey talk to him, did he obey the will of the Lord. (Numbers chapter 22)

YOUR CHALLENGE

Well, if you're not careful, the same kind of thing that happened to Balaam can get hold of you, and it won't let go. I've seen people willing to allow something to get hold of them, and the next thing you know prayer is a memory.

I've known guys so ugly they couldn't buy a date get pulled out of prayer by a woman. This one guy I knew would virtually chain himself to a post in prayer and say, "I'm never going to leave this post, Tim. I'm chained here for life." He was committed to prayer every day, and doing it faithfully. You could have threatened to kill him, and he wouldn't have quit praying. You could have shot him between the eyes, and he would have just kept praying.

Then the Devil began to orchestrate his song of seduction. A beautiful little thing from the southern hemisphere would come along, walk through the door, and give him a little talk with her eyes. The next thing I knew he was telling me, "Brother Tim, Brother Tim, here's the dream woman of my life! My dreams are coming true, this is of God. God is so faithful."

The Devil is drawing him off with his Balaam. Your Balaam is whatever draws you off; something you enjoy so much that you can't spend time with God. I don't doubt God's ability to send him a wife, but if something consumes you, and you don't pray any longer, it's dangerous. I've seen people lose absolutely all drive and commitment to prayer, and the things God called them to do, when something—or someone—gets hold of them.

I've seen young women come to church, get committed to Jesus, love Jesus, and all of a sudden some devil in blue jeans walks through the door. He's attracted to her because she's saved and turned on to Jesus, but he's rotten to the core. And the next thing you know, she's "feeling led" that he is an answer to prayer.

She's going to follow him, because she's made the decision this is the one God has sent. So, she gets on that donkey of emotion and starts to ride. Her whole family, and everybody she knows begins to say, "You know, this is not God, this is not good for you, it's not healthy." But, no matter what you say, she's not listening. It's just like what happened to Balaam.

I'm telling you, if I'm walking down the road one day, and my dog Bud looks up and says, "I think we better stop here, we're going the wrong direction," I'm going to stop. I'm not going to beat him. I'm not going to say, "Shut up Bud," and keep walking. No, what I'm going to do is stop and say, "Bud, is that you?" In fact, I might even say, "Devil,..." because people who talk to animals get into trouble, or at least Adam and Eve did with a snake. If my dog starts to talk to me, I'm going to listen.

Can you imagine it? This woman is jogging down the road, trying to catch up to her dream guy, when her German Shepherd at her side begins to speak, and says, "Listen, stop, you're going in the wrong direction." But, instead of stopping, she starts beating her dog, saying, "Shut up, dog, I see him, he's ahead of me, I'm going to catch him." She doesn't care if her dog talks, if her pastor talks, if her mamma talks, or if every friend she has talks; all she wants to do is go on down that road and catch him.

Now she doesn't have a hold of *him*, he's got a hold of her. That's the difference. See, God doesn't mind you having something, He just doesn't want that something to have you.

FROM GOD'S POINT OF VIEW

Jesus told me, "I don't mind money. I don't mind you having money. I just don't want the money to have you." When the money gets you, or the person gets you, then it controls you instead of you controlling it. I know how dangerous it can be, once that thing gets ahold of you. Forty coal trucks was a big temptation.

You've seen people who are in a good marriage, and then something gets ahold of them and they let it break their marriage. No matter what you say to them, they just won't listen to you.

Here's what Scripture has to say about the struggle to be faithful, and to resist the temptations of the Devil.

He that is faithful in that which is least is faithful also in much: and he that is unjust in the least is unjust also in much.

If therefore ye have not been faithful in the unrighteous mammon, who will commit to your trust the true riches?

And if ye have not been faithful in that which is another man's, who shall give you that which is your own?

No servant can serve two masters: for either he will hate the one, and love the other; or else he will hold to the one, and despise the other. Ye cannot serve God and mammon.

Luke 16:10-13

CHAPTER 8
CHOSEN FOR ASSIGNMENT

Another way to understand this conflict over money is from God's point of view.

For the kingdom of heaven is as a man traveling into a far country, who called his own servants, and delivered unto them his goods.

And unto one he gave five talents, to another two, and to another one;...

Matthew 25:14-15

So, in other words, he gave each one a certain amount of money. When he returned, he inspected them.

His Lord said unto him, Well done, thou good and faithful servant: thou hast been faithful over a few things, I will make thee ruler over many things: enter thou into the joy of thy lord.

Matthew 25:21

Here the Word comes back to the issue of faithfulness. God looks at your faithfulness to Him and His ways. Faithfulness with your money; faithfulness in your prayer life, and faithfulness in the assignment He has given you, no matter how small. The Scripture says, **"...for many be called, but few chosen."** (Matthew 20:16) You may indeed have the call of God on your life, but never be chosen by Him for an assignment if you can't be faithful in the things of your life. The key is faithfulness.

What the Lord does is give you a starter assignment, and then sees how faithful you are in it. In addition, He looks to see how faithful you are in your family, your job, and He takes those things into account before He assigns you something new.

How big an assignment the Lord gives you is also dependent on how much pressure you can stand. If they wrote a bunch of negative books about you, what kind of pressure would that bring into your life? What if you had people trying to bring down your ministry? The Devil will try to divide your house against itself so it can't stand. He'll try to get somebody, a weak link within your organization or your family, to cause you trouble. He knows that unforgiveness will get you in trouble with God. In order to be chosen for bigger and bigger assignments you must be able to stand in faithfulness under those kinds of pressures.

Remember the list the Lord gave me? I had to close the door to the Devil, and that's what the list was for. The list was what the Lord used to show me the areas in my life where I'd left the door open to the Devil. The number one thing on the list was faithfulness, and a key area of faithfulness was money.

The Lord said, "If you're not faithful in money, I can't use you." I was somewhat surprised that he'd even mention money.

"Money doesn't control me," I answered.

Well, about six months later He said, "I want you to go to Los Angeles."

I said, "I can't go to Los Angeles."

"Why?"

"Because, I don't have any money," I said.

And the Lord said, "I thought money didn't tell you what you could and couldn't do for Me. Now if you're unfaithful in that, I can't send you where I want you."

Well, He had me nailed on that one, and I had to change my thinking. I had been committed to faithfulness in tithing because I'd learned there are some pretty specific promises made to those who tithe. Scripture says the windows of heaven are open over the tither. The devourer [Satan] is rebuked for the tither's sake, and God's blessings come in due season unhindered by the enemy. I had learned to trust God in all that was due to me as a tither (see Malachi 3:10-11), and I'd passed on the coal trucks temptation, but now the Lord was requiring that I become faithful in my attitudes toward money as well.

In the world money represents power, but if you depend on money to put you over, you're headed for real trouble. It is not the solution to all your needs and problems. If you operate your life or your ministry like money is the answer, the Lord will take you to a place in your life where the power of money cannot do what you need to do for yourself or God. You see, the power of money can't heal you; it can't buy the anointing that causes a backslider to come back to God. But let me tell you, the power of God can heal and restore. God wants to take you beyond the power of money and into His power.

SETTING THE STANDARD

As I've mentioned, you may have the call of God on your life, but never receive an assignment from God to fulfill that call. You might be called as a pastor, but never be assigned a church to pastor. Now you might go pastor anyway, without a Divine assignment from God, but that's a work started in the flesh. God has no obligation to sustain a work like that.

You say, "Well, God will send me somewhere when I'm ready." That's true, but you'll find God will first require you to meet certain standards. If He makes the deacons meet certain standards before He uses them, and they are the table servers, He obviously isn't going to make them clean up their act and let the other ministries go wild (1 Timothy 3 & Titus 1). It's a fact: before God can use you, you must learn to meet a certain standard of maturity. First Timothy chapter 3 isn't only a standard of character, it's also a standard of maturity.

YOUR BOTTOM LINE

The bottom line of this can be summarized in these four statements.

1. If you can't surrender to His will, He won't allow people to surrender to you.
2. If you won't submit, He won't have people submit to you.
3. If you're not willing to change, He won't let you change someone else.
4. If you can't whip the Devil in your own life, you are not going to be able to whip him in someone else's.

It's not that God creates hardship in our lives, but He looks at how well you handle the pressures. James says, *"...the trying of your faith worketh patience. But let patience have her perfect work, that ye may be perfect and entire, wanting nothing.* (James 1:3-4)

You must be faithful over little before He will make you ruler over much. (Matthew 25:21 author's paraphrase).

THE NEXT ASSIGNMENT

When I began to prove myself faithful in finances the Lord moved me on to my next assignment...prayer. He said, "I want you to pray a certain amount each day."

So, I made the decision to pray. Every morning I'd pray, and I'll tell you, the first four or five months, it was the hardest thing I ever did. The spirit was willing, but the flesh was weak. You'll find you don't *want* to get up and pray, but you have to *make* yourself do it.

I'm telling you, I was so determined not to mess up on my prayer assignment. I had made a quality decision to be a man of prayer if that was what the Lord wanted. So, I continued to pray because I had made the decision to be faithful to the assignment God had given me.

Then the Lord called me to pastor. We planted a church in a small town. The church had about 300 people in attendance. We were doing really well. Everybody loved me; in fact, I couldn't find anyone who didn't like me. Donna and I would be doing our grocery shopping and we'd meet somebody at the meat counter. Next thing you know, we're going out to lunch with them. Donna would say, "You don't know them." I would reply, "I don't know if I know them or not, but I sure like them, don't you?"

I remember visiting somebody, and they said, "Now, don't let him out there around mean old Uncle Henry. Uncle Henry is crazy, and he's got his dog out there with him. Don't you go out there, Brother Tim." The next thing you know, I'd be out there witnessing to Uncle Henry, while he worked on his pickup. We'd have him in church on Sunday morning, and get him and his dog saved, because I was just walking in the love of Jesus. Every person that I met loved me. I used to joke that, "Even I like me".

We began doing local television, and after a year we had our own equipment and our own production people. We were doing radio all over the state of Oregon, and began preparing to do a national television program with Trinity Broadcasting Network.

All these good things were happening because we were faithful to pray in the Spirit and spend time with God every day.

See, it's one thing to know a lot *about* God, but it's another to *know* Him.

Prayer brings you into the place where you know Him. Because I spent time every day in the Word and prayer and began to have fellowship with God, He would speak to me. He would warn me at times to avoid certain people or to avoid certain things. Other times, He would guide me to the right people. Everything I put my hand to prospered.

THE ATTACK

Then, out of nowhere, I heard my brother had died. So, I went back to Virginia. I drove straight through from Oregon. It took about 50 hours, and then I spent another two or three days at the funeral. We're mainly Irish, and at an Irish funeral they stay up for days at a time. They bring the casket into the home or into the church, and have a wake. You're up all night, all the next day, and the next, and maybe you'll sleep a little bit. I was so tired I hadn't had time to pray.

After several days in Virginia, a local family member called me. They told me my brother's daughter was going to commit suicide. "You need to come, Tim," they pleaded. "You're the only one who can help. You're the only one who knows what to say to keep her from killing herself."

So, of course, I went, and she didn't commit suicide.

Well, by the time the crisis had passed, I'd been out of prayer for three weeks. But, because there had been a death in the family, and a near suicide with my niece, I excused myself.

Just as I was getting ready to return to our church in Oregon my grandfather died. Now if I wanted to remain a McFall, I had to stay in Virginia. And to tell you the truth, I wanted to be there, so I stayed. I had been gone about a month, and by the time I got back home, all hell had broken loose.

THE LAZARUS TEMPTATION

The Devil had offered me the Balaam temptation, the coal trucks, and I wouldn't go for it, but I did fall for the Lazarus temptation. Let me explain.

Jesus loved Lazarus very much, and He wanted to go to him when He heard he had become sick and was dying. But Jesus, speaking by faith, told His disciples in John 11:4 that Lazarus was not unto death.

Then Jesus waited another two days. The reason He waited was because He stayed in prayer.

When you stay in prayer, as you start to listen to God, it's like walking during the daylight. When you walk during the day, you hear from God, and your path is clear. When you walk during the night, that is in prayerlessness, you'll stumble, because you can't see where you're going. (John 11:9-10)

Two days go by and Jesus tells His disciples He wants to go into Judaea. The disciples are more than concerned. They knew the Jews wanted to stone Him. In fact, the Jews had tried to run Jesus out of town the last time He was there. He would have been killed if He hadn't slipped through the crowd to keep from being stoned. Because He knew the circumstances were hazardous, He wouldn't come out of prayer.

In fact, it was so dangerous one disciple, in a moment of ministerial bravado declared, *"Let us also go, that we may die with Him."* (John 11:16) But Jesus stayed in prayer, in spite of the pleas of Lazarus' family and the pressure of His own circumstances, and was able to move in God's will and timing.

A "Lazarus" is someone who needs help, but you must come out of prayer to give it. The mechanics of ministry can choke God right out of you, if you let them. Most people will sell out for their own version of a bowl of stew, just like Esau did (Genesis 25:29-34). It doesn't take 40 coal trucks for them to feel the pressure of temptation. Sadly, all it takes is a little bit of television, a little bit of money, a little bit of tragedy, or a little bit of something else instead of praying.

What you have to understand is, there are times when you must put prayer before everything else. When you're in prayer with God, God will let you know when those times are. Prayer has to be number one. And though I had made that commitment earlier, I had walked away from it because of a need that was drastic. I let myself fall out of prayer for a month.

NO PRAYER, NO PEACE

Let me tell you, I wasn't prepared for what was going to take place on my return. The church was torn apart. Nobody liked me anymore. In fact, I got to where I didn't even like myself anymore. There were so many spiritual fires burning it was taking all my time just running from one to the other, trying to put them out. All because I had come out of prayer.

God came to me again. He said, "I want you to prove yourself faithful in prayer." So I prayed. I made the decision to pray, and more than that, I wasn't going to come out of prayer. I was holding to that, no matter what.

Suddenly, the ministry began to turn around and, though it took years of prayer and hard work, it finally came back to what it had been. My secret weapon had been prayer. But now I was to learn the next lesson, the lesson of obedience...the hard way.

CHAPTER 9
LEARNING THE HARD WAY

I don't particularly like telling the following story. It's a bit embarrassing. It is, however, the best way I know to illustrate the point of this chapter; a point you must grasp if the Lord is ever going to use you effectively for His service.

When we talk about closing the door to the Devil the reality is, until we have a heart to hear the Lord when He speaks, we can never function confidently in our obedience. Here's the story.

* * *

One Saturday night, I was driving around with my son, and the Lord told me, "Go back to the house." His voice was very clear and I had no doubt it was the Lord. Why I replied the way I did, I don't know. I can only suppose I thought I understood something about my schedule that God didn't. Like He was limited in His understanding or something.

"I don't have time, I have to leave tomorrow," I said. I was headed out of town on a ministry trip the following day and still had several things to do before I left. I felt really pressed for time.

"Pull over," the Lord said, short and clear.

But we didn't pull over and kept on going.

"Buckle up," He said.

I wouldn't buckle up either.

Again, **"Buckle up!"** This time it was a command.

I still wouldn't do it.

This was before the law required you to wear a seat belt. It was night, and there was no traffic but, incredibly, I looked at my son and said, "I should buckle up."

"Yeah, you should," he agreed.

"I should buckle up," I said again.

"You *should* buckle up, Dad."

But I didn't do it.

Then, suddenly, out of nowhere came a car driven by a thoroughly drunk lady. It was headed straight for us and we could not avoid her. We hit head on!

It took four operations for me to recover from that accident. God didn't cause it: He wasn't behind it, but because I was out of prayer and fellowship with Him, I was vulnerable to the attack. I couldn't recognize the Lord's warnings for what they were. Now, when I look back on it, I can't see how I could have missed them, but I did.

RECOVERY

Needless to say, I went back into regular prayer. Not praying was no longer an option for me. But since I wouldn't pray when it was easier, I got to learn the discipline of prayer under the most difficult of circumstances.

I woke up in a hospital bed pumped full of medications. I'll tell you one thing for sure: one of the hardest things I ever did was try to pray when I was on that medication. Over the next several days I healed up some and hurt lots.

Hospital food being what hospital food usually is, I asked my daughter to bring me a Big Mac, if she could. She brought me the hamburger and, after I finished it, the nurse came and gave me a shot of pain killer. Almost immediately, I became violently sick.

To make matters worse, I had to stand with my head straight up because they had operated on the back of my neck, and it was still stiff. Basically, I ended up redecorating the walls in my own room. It took a second shot before they figured out it was the medication that was making me so sick.

They put me on Tylenol then. It didn't help the pain as much but at least my head was clear enough to pray. Even though I was supposed to be in the hospital for five to six days, I was released the next day.

INTO THE FIELD

After a while of almost constant prayer, Jesus said to me, "Now that you've proven yourself faithful in prayer, I'm going to assign some work to you."

"Oh, boy! What am I going to do?"

"Next year," He said, "I want you to hold 20 crusades."

I was thinking, *"Wow, that's not bad, travel and hold 20 crusades."* I felt excited.

But, instead of asking the Lord for the how-to's and the particulars, I had my own ideas, which I expressed emphatically to the Lord.

"I'm not calling anybody! I'm not going to cross that line. They'll have to call me."

"Listen," the Lord said, "if they were hearing from Me that well, I wouldn't even need to send you. I'm going to send you to some places where they don't even know My voice. In fact, they hardly even know Me. They are not going to like it while you are there, and they are not going to like you. But, I'm sending you there and I want you to obey Me."

"Okay. Yes, Sir. You want me to call, we'll call; we'll get this going." (Notice I didn't say I, I said we).

So I recruited a lady who could have sold ice to Eskimos and screen doors to the submarine service. This woman could sell! I hired her to get these meetings booked. She started working and worked her way through all my lists of contacts, and could only get one meeting booked for me. Everybody loved this lady, but the problem was, they just didn't *"feel led"* to have me.

I knew the truth. I didn't like it, but I knew it. I had to do the calling myself. I had to get over my pride. Remember, I told Jesus I wouldn't make phone calls. Jesus said I needed to obey Him and do what He said to do, regardless of what other people thought, or even what I thought I had been called to do.

So I started calling all my friends who had said they'd love to have me come and minister. But now no one would have me. I started to panic. It was so bad, it was embarrassing. I didn't care who it was, where it was, what church, or what gathering. I finally began to say, "You know, I can bring my own offering if you let me come and say something." I was prepared to do whatever it took to get through the door. I begged and I pleaded.

I remember one of the meetings: 13 people were there and I received a $7.00 offering. I paid my own travel expenses and motel. I didn't care.

I had learned to follow the advice of Oral Roberts. He said, "Find out what God wants you to do, and get it done at all costs. Take care of the job. Be faithful in it." I knew God meant business. When the Lord tells you something, you do it. I know, it's not always pleasant, but do it anyway.

THE UNFORGETTABLE 19TH

The day of the 19th service, I went out and ate a light lunch with my wife Donna and we headed home to rest up before the service that night. As I was driving I had a tachycardia, the kind where your heart beats over 200 times a minute. It doesn't pump the blood, it just sort of quivers. Consequently, the blood didn't flow through me very well. When the attack came I kept thinking, *"If I can just relax, this thing will settle back down."* But there was nothing I could do with my mind to control my heart.

I went to the hospital where my son-in-law and my daughter were working in the emergency room. When they came out and realized my heart was not beating normally, they talked me into letting a doctor see me.

"Daddy, you can die from this," they said. I was almost unconscious at that point.

So I finally went in. When you're getting into your late 30's, and you're perspiring and having chest problems, they take you real seriously. They threw me down on a table and went to work on me. They tried to get needles into me. They tried everywhere but because my heart wasn't beating properly, they couldn't find a vein.

Then they rolled this big machine in, and I heard a noise that sounded like a jet engine. Two nurses came over to the table I was on and started to strap my arms down. You know, it's a funny thing, when they strap down the arms of a man who's having chest problems, you have to wonder. I looked over at the big machine and then at my daughter, and said, "What is that?"

"That's for you," she said.

"Oh, in case my heart stops or something?"

"No, no, they're going to have to stop your heart, Dad. Then they're going to restart it."

That's when I started to panic. "What? What! Somebody pray, get a hold of my wife and let her pray. Dear God, whatever she wants to say, let her pray! Somebody pray!"

I'm telling you, by this time, I was going berserk. The reason they strap your arms down is they don't want to start the shock treatment and have you reach out and grab someone while you're still conscious. They were all ready to go ahead with the shock machine when, all of a sudden, one of them screamed out, "He's converted, he's converted on his own!" And I felt my heart go back to normal.

I didn't know what they meant, but I began to yell, over and over, "I'm converted! I'm converted! I'm converted!" I began to cry, and the doctor came running in a few seconds later. He snapped his fingers like, "Wow, I missed this one." In fact, I think he was looking forward to stopping and restarting me. I don't know about you, but I don't like that stopping business. People whose hearts have stopped, they usually die.

MIRACLE SERVICE

I had a miracle service scheduled for that night, and I was tempted with not going. After my emotional experience at the hospital and a brush with death, I concluded it would be wiser to stay at home. After a short discussion with my wife we both felt it was best to complete service 19, since I had said I'd be there. Psalms 15:4 talks about the man who swears to his own hurt, and changes not. I wanted to be that man because I wanted to be faithful to what God had given me to do.

So Donna and a friend loaded me into the pickup and took me home to take a shower, because I was a mess. She cleaned me up, got me ready, loaded me back up into the pickup, and our friend took me over to the service. I came staggering in, and everyone was thinking, "Wow, he's really anointed!" The truth was, I was so weak I could barely stand up. I had no choice but to say, "God, listen. You've got to do something or I'm in trouble."

Now I could see not much had happened in the previous 18 services, but let me tell you, somewhere in the middle of this one, God began to move. It was one of the greatest miracle services I have ever had. People were healed, set free, delivered and baptized in the Holy Ghost. God jumped up and shined in His glory.

Why?

Because I had proven myself faithful.

Since that time, the phone has been ringing off the hook. The next year we did about 50 crusades, and had a list of people waiting for us to come when we could. From that time I've never lacked for having a crusade.

If you prove yourself faithful in the Lord, then the Lord will assign you a bigger task. But, you must prove yourself faithful...first.

CHAPTER 10
GIANTS IN THE LAND

If God exalts you, nothing can stop you. But, if you do it your way, you're guaranteed by the Word of God to be brought down. Most people are looking for a man to put them over. Even if you were able to position yourself, promote yourself, and politic your way up through the system, if you lift yourself up, it's guaranteed you're going to drop like a hot rock. Even if you can manipulate yourself into a prominent position, and side-step all the personalities on your pathway to success, you're merely the second shoe waiting to drop.

If you're waiting for a man to do something for you, you're waiting for the wrong person. In fact, you'll find yourself fitting into the world's system instead of doing it God's way. God wants to show Himself strong on our behalf. He wants people who won't be moved by circumstances, people who will stand in faith as they face the giants in the Promised Land.

Oh, you mean you didn't know there were giants in your Promised Land? Nobody told you? Well, of course there are. Israel had them and so do we. If somebody told you there were no giants in the Promised Land, they lied. But as soon as you start to move into the things of God, the storms will come. They don't come from God, but they will come.

The easiest way to cope with the challenge is to stay outside the Promised Land. Trust me, the giants will be there, and if you don't have a relationship with Jesus, you will fail. So why not start out right; let's do it God's way.

THE DEVIL'S TACTIC

What the Devil sets out to do is deceive you. The worst part is, if he succeeds, you'll never know you've been deceived. The angels were created to do nothing but obey God, and yet the Devil was able to take one third of them with him in his mutiny. He takes on personality. It's like going down to the car dealer and pretty soon you have to call 911 to get away from the salesman because he has become so personable. You don't know how you've been had, but you've been had.

You know, Eve was one smart woman. She and Adam were able to name all the animals and keep all the names in their heads. They weren't down at the water hole one day and Adam saying, "Honey, what did we name that little striped one? You know, about this high. What did we call him again?"

"Zebra."

"Oh yeah, that's right, I forgot."

She was one smart woman. It's a fact that we only use 10 to 15 percent of our brain. She used 100 percent, and the Devil was *still* able to deceive her. Then he was able to cause Adam to commit high treason.

The Devil will use a frontal assault combined with deception like he did with the Apostle Paul. Paul was the man who wrote Romans 8 and two thirds of the books of the New Testament, who prayed more than any of us, who walked with God, who knew Him to the point that God had to catch him up to heaven and give him a revelation.

The Devil drove him nearly to distraction with harassments. He was shipwrecked twice, stoned several times, whipped and more. Finally, it dawned on him that this wasn't just bad luck. Nobody has that kind of bad luck. If even the Apostle Paul could be deceived, how much more do we need to be praying?

The Devil doesn't let anybody slip through. You get tried on level A, B, C, D, and E. If you don't know how to back him off, he's going to be right there working on you. He's going to try you on every level. And deception is his principle weapon.

I WANTED TO QUIT

For years, in the middle of the week I used to feel like I wanted to quit church. I didn't even want to go on Sunday. I wanted to go fishing; I wanted to go somewhere else, anywhere else. I was deceived. I didn't realize it was an attack. I would succumb to the attack, not knowing it was a spiritual battle. You know, if I had known that the Devil was trying me, I would have done much better. There should have been a little sign that popped up and said, "Test has begun." I had to learn to break the Devil's hold on me, or pretty soon I'd have a church full of fishermen like myself, not saints.

The Devil comes to where you are in your thinking, with his deceptively charming and persuasive personality, and moves right in. Then he begins to manipulate you. He doesn't try to annihilate you, all he's attempting to do is to *"neutralize"* you. He wants to get you to say, "I know prayer works," but you're not praying; "I believe in the Word," but you're not acting on the Word.

The Devil has assigned deceptive spiritual activity to stop you and he has a plan. For some of us, he has a six hour plan. For some of us he needs six days. Some of us he knows will take six months, and some of us it will take six years, but he has a plan to stop each of us.

If he can get you out of prayer, then the Holy Spirit can't stop the attack, and you might as well face it, you're going to have a fight on your hands. There *are* giants in the land.

Have you ever lost your appetite for the Word? When you lose that hunger you've been whipped. There was a time we could have shot you between the eyes, and you still would have shown up for prayer. Now we can't drag you into the prayer closet.

If the Devil can't deceive you quite so easily, he then begins to offer you things. You might say, "The Devil has never offered me anything." Well, I hate to be the one to tell you, but if that's true, you probably haven't been very serious about prayer. You get serious and he'll offer you something. If he has to, he'll offer you everything...he did Jesus. If you'll accept money, you'll find money. If you'll accept men, he'll find you one. If you'll accept women, he'll find you one.

Some say, "You know, I've just gotten married, so I can't show up for prayer". Even being a new bride is no excuse for staying away from prayer and the Word. Another says, "I have a job, I have the affairs of life." None of those excuses, nor a hundred more, are valid.

BEING LED BY THE HOLY SPIRIT

The Word says those who are led by the Spirit of God are the sons of God (Romans 8:14). In other words, Paul is saying that for you to walk with God, you must listen to, and be led by, the Holy Spirit. If you are going to manifest the love and life of God, you're going to have to hear from the Holy Spirit. You can't simply quote God's Word without a Divine connection to God Himself, and expect to be led by the Spirit of God.

Power *requires* the Divine connection. When you make the connection, then you will start to hear from God. You cannot walk in the flesh and cause spiritual things to happen. You must walk in the Spirit to cause spiritual things to happen. Only then will they happen in the flesh.

Have you figured it out? When you start to pray the Devil gets nervous, and if you continue, he doesn't like you anymore. But everything of God must first be established in the spiritual realm through prayer before it will manifest in the natural realm.

I find a lot of people with a call of God on their lives, but they haven't been chosen to do a thing, because they have not applied themselves in the spiritual realm where it counts. They're out there trying to manipulate. They're out there trying to politic and position themselves. They understand self-promotion as an art. If you understand those three "P's" you might go far in the religious world. There are handbooks on how to promote, how to position, and how to politic yourself in the Christian world.

But, remember what the Scripture says, *"Except the Lord build the house, they labour in vain that build it:..."* (Psalms 127:1)

THIS TIME I DID QUIT

One time I did quit. I walked into the house and said, "That's it, I quit, I'm not going any further. God will work the daylights out of you. He'll rebuke you for trying to die, take your last two pennies, and your last bit of food and then ask you to live by faith. I quit!" Before I could say another word, I felt about 100 and some pounds jump on my back. It was my wife, and she was screaming like a wild woman, "Come out of him, Devil. Come out of him in the Name of Jesus."

Don't you know I wanted to turn around and straighten her out, but she continued to pray. I hollered, "Don't talk to me that way!" She said, "I'm not talking to you, I'm talking to the Devil!" By the time I did turn around, I had to admit I did feel much better. I came to my senses and said, "I'm sorry, I'm having a bad day." I felt plagued by bad luck but, in fact, the Devil had moved in. I thought it was me.

The Devil has deceived a lot smarter people than me. He's even neutralized an entire army. Frankly, I'm afraid not to pray, because prayer and the Word are the only weapons we have against spiritual attacks.

Anybody I know, who is doing anything for Jesus, has proved

themselves in the prayer realm. To the degree that Jesus says, "You can be trusted now, you won't be moved," He can assign work to you. When you have been found faithful in the realm of prayer, then God will choose you for an assignment.

Oh, you might go out and do something yourself because the call is there, and you'll say, "I'm called, I think I'm going to go do something," but haven't you noticed God hasn't chosen you to take the city yet? Until you learn to whip the Devil over yourself, you're not going to be able to whip the Devil off anyone else, let alone take your city. And don't be deceived, the Devil on your spouse is not your problem...it's the one on you.

JESUS AND PRAYER

Jesus wants to use you in the Kingdom more than you want to be used. He's not playing hard to get. He's not saying, "You know, I don't think I like you; I like Oral Roberts better." The Devil that's working on your wife is no problem. The Devil that's working on your church is no problem. The Devil that's working on your city is no problem, *if* you turn Jesus, your intercessor, loose, and allow Him to take care of the Devil.

The Devil will try to steal prayer from you because he's not trying to stop you, he's trying to stop Jesus in you.

If he can stop you from praying, he has stopped Jesus from taking the city. Haven't you noticed how the more you pray in the spirit, the more revival we have?

If it comes down to a choice between prayer or something else, make prayer your number one priority. Here's how it works. Wherever you put Jesus in your life is where you're going to come out. You put Him last, you're going to come in last. If you put your children first, then your children will end up living like the Devil. But if you put Jesus first, He'll take care of your children. God understands the concept of a chain of command, and because Jesus was obedient to His command, He honors you when you are obedient to Jesus' commands.

THE LAZARUS TEMPTATION

But can you resist the pull of the Lazarus, "The one who you love needs you." Jesus wouldn't come out of prayer to go to Lazarus, because He knew it was a set-up. After Lazarus died all the Jews left, because they figured Jesus wouldn't come back after the man had been wrapped and mummified. They all went home and said, "He won't show up now, they've got him mummified, no way to get him out now."

Understand, to prepare Lazarus for burial they would take a pitcher of resin and strips of cloth, and once they had soaked them in the resin, they would wrap his body in them. It would harden like a cast, and stick to the body like glue. That's why the Jews were so sure Jesus wouldn't show up.

Do you have what it takes to stay in prayer and obey God? If not, then you are being bought off by something. We know a pastor who had 20 people and was going under. He was working a secular job to pay his bills, and nobody was concerned for him...until we got him into this kind of prayer. Now he's running a large crowd of people. They're taking one city, and the last time I talked to him they're in the process of taking another one. His problem is different now.

But all his friends are now telling him he's getting a little too far off the beam because he's putting too much emphasis on prayer.

How concerned would you be for a guy who had Jesus on his side like that? I tell you, I like that. I believe I'm going to let Jesus take care of some situations in my life. In fact, I've been doing that for awhile.

You say, "How long will it take?"

I don't know. Your job is to pray until it's done. If you're going to move into God, pray what you know to pray for, and be obedient to what He tells you. He will expect you to obey. If you'll do that, He'll take care of you. You won't have to worry. He says, "If you seek the kingdom of God first, you won't have to worry about what the Gentiles are seeking after. All of these things will be added unto you." (Matthew 6:33 author's paraphrase) If you put God first, I guarantee He'll start to take care of your children, your job, your money. When you start to pray, you become dangerous to the Devil.

SO......WHAT DO I DO?

You say, "Jesus, what do I do?"
Do you know what He said to me?
"Nothing. Don't do anything."
"Should I go to a city?"
"Don't go anywhere, don't make a move yet. I don't want you to do anything but come to Me. The only direction you're to go is toward Me."

Some of you haven't figured that out yet. You go to prayer and you're wondering why God hasn't told you to go build the City of Faith, or some such grand assignment. It is because you haven't allowed Him to build it yet in the Spirit. When He gets it done in the Spirit, He'll send you to go do it in the natural.

THE JUDAS TEMPTATION

I want to add, "And watch out for those who kiss you on the cheek and tell you how much they love you." The Devil will always try to place a Judas right in the middle of your mess. Most of us have fallen for him a time or two, because he loves us and, of course, we want to be loved. At the most critical time, your Judas will turn on you and, if you're not careful, he'll bring down the ministry. Your ministry becomes "at risk" when you stop praying, and try to take care of things in the flesh.

If those who surround you in ministry don't pray, they are dangerous to you. I don't trust anybody who doesn't pray; I don't care how much they kiss me and tell me they love me. It's hard to turn down some guy that has just sowed $70,000 into your ministry and wants to go to dinner with you. However, there is a big difference between being supported financially by someone who has heard from God and having your influence bought.

The Devil doesn't try to take you from where you are to where he wants you to be immediately; it's a progression he's working on. He starts out offering you something small in the beginning. He'll tell you it won't hurt to miss prayer a little bit, because you can always make it up later. No harm in missing once, right? If he can stop you from praying, he stops Jesus from standing in the gap over you, and then you become an open prey. See the choice?

You *pray*, or you become *prey*.

You say, "How much should I pray?"

How much of Jesus do you want? Even sleep can be a temptation (Matthew 26:40-41). I'm not talking about turning down $70,000; but how many of you have ever turned down sleep? Jesus wants to use you more than you want to be used. He wants you to have more than you've ever dreamed of having. Some of you have been called to do great things for the kingdom of God, and you're sleeping through it.

If you will arouse yourself and begin to pray, God will be faithful to point out any Judas in your midst.

THE HARDEST AREA

The hardest area for preachers to break free in is money, trusting God for money.

Some of you have been called to do millions and millions of dollars worth of work for the Lord, but God can't release it to you until the hold that money has over you is broken in your life.

I was praying one day, and I saw this big hand stick out of heaven, and God said, "Give me some."

"No, Jesus," I said, "you didn't get it right, I'm the guy who has the macaroni and cheese, the cans of tuna and evaporated milk. *I'm the guy who needs the money.*"

Again He said, "Give Me some. If you have a need, then start to sow. The widow who gave two mites gave more than them all, because she gave from the heart. The rest of them gave out of their abundance; they didn't give out of trust" (Mark 12:42-44 author's paraphrase)

The best thing we could do for some of you is come and take all your money so you'd *have* to trust God. But, because you have just enough money to hang on, you never cross over into the realm of trusting God so much that, if He doesn't come through, you're in trouble. If you think about it, most of you are in some sort of financial trouble anyway, so why not trust God completely and get out of it.

THE TRUTH IS...

The truth is, until God gets your money, He doesn't have you. If money has power, and you trust in it, then He can't send you to do the work, because Luke 16:11 says, **"If therefore ye have not been faithful in the unrighteous mammon, who will commit to your trust the true riches?"**

But some of you have been trained by the best, in what I call the "martial arts" of not giving. The best have tried, and you've succeeded in fighting off their attempt to receive an offering from you. Somebody mentions money and you shut down right there. So the best thing we could do for you is come over to your house this afternoon, take all your food and all your money, and leave you where you have to say, "Oh God, I've got to trust You." You've been giving out of abundance, instead of true trust.

When you start to trust Jesus, somebody will try to withhold your money, but let me tell you, Jesus is big enough to send the angels to get it for you.

But if you hang onto the little bit you have, and that's all you have, just enough to survive, you're in survival mode. If one meal is all you have and you won't give it, then that's all you'll ever have.

Some of you are down to one meal, and it's stopping the blessings of God, because that's all you can see. But read 1 Kings chapter 17 (author's paraphrase). Here the prophet Elijah asked a destitute widow for part of her very last bit of food. She gave it to him in faith and, from then on, she never lacked meal or oil.

If you want your oil pot and meal barrel to fill up, you'll have to be willing to give up that little meagerly amount of food you have. Can you do it? If you can, then He can use you to bless others with His provision.

CHAPTER 11
BOLT THE DOOR

Someone asked me recently, "Is it any easier to pray after 20 years?"

No! It's just as hard now to get up early in the morning as it was 20 years ago. Sometimes my flesh says, "No, we're not getting up today, we're going to rest." It's amazing what your mind comes up with to get you out of prayer. You didn't know you were so sharp, or had so many good ideas, until you went in to pray.

Sad to say, most of us get bought off, or beaten, by the simplest of things. When you go to pray, there's going to be a million things to do, but if you don't do what needs to be done in the spirit, there is no sense in working in the flesh. The work of the ministry is always done in the Spirit before it's done in the natural. Your commitment to that principle will make all the difference. But beyond that, there is also the matter of a solid knowledge base.

WE NEED MORE

Before God can build you into someone He can use, you must have a solid base of knowledge of the Word and of His ways. It's important that you receive that.

Also important is receiving knowledge by revelation. The Apostle Paul said there is the form of prophecy, and there is revelation

(1 Corinthians 14:6). Paul says he went up to Jerusalem by revelation (Galations 2:1-2). You can receive direction by revelation. But there is no sense getting any direction if you don't have anything to go with. There is no sense in God taking you and throwing you in the middle of something you're not trained for; you won't last a day.

Take the jungle warfare training I did for example. They turned us loose in the jungle training area, and we didn't last 30 minutes, because we weren't trained for it yet. That part of the training was designed to show you how stupid you were. We'd trip on things we never saw coming until we were slamming into the ground. You must be prepared before He sends you to do the work. "Many be called, but few chosen." (Matthew 20:16) because they don't meet certain spiritual criteria, or a certain maturity. Jesus told me there was a number of things I needed to get out of my life, and if I would, He could send me.

KNOWLEDGE, REVELATION, DIRECTION

In Ephesians we find there's a spirit of revelation of God's Word and direction for life. God uses revelation to give direction. An example of revelation in God's Word is when Peter understood that Jesus was the Christ. He didn't receive the revelation knowledge from man, but he received that knowledge from God. (Matthew 16:16 author's paraphrase)

But, what most of us need, instead of direction, is a change in how we pray. We are not going to pray God into our will; we are going to pray ourselves into His will. That's where we will have success. We will not put God in a box and formulate something to make Him go our way. If there is any changing to be done, it will be us, praying ourselves into His will.

What you'll find, as you start to pray, is that God will begin to speak to you and deal with the areas which are causing you trouble, through revelation. If your doctrine is wrong, He'll show you how to correct it. He can't send you until He gets your doctrine right. He's not going to send you to the masses to mess them up.

You say, "But I pray all the time."

I don't care if you pray 16 hours a day, if your doctrine is wrong, you're in trouble; the Devil will wipe you out. Somebody will come along and tell you, "Well, don't you know it's all going to work out for your good?" in reference to Romans 8:28. But you'll find in Romans 8:5-6 that if you are carnal, nothing will work out to your good; except that, when you die, you're going to heaven. (author's paraphrase)

If you are carnally minded it will lead to death, because what you sow, you will reap. When you connect up with God, and you listen to God, you receive direction from Him. Only then will things begin to work out. But you *must* listen to God.

THE REAL YOU

In Luke 12:1 Jesus talked about the hypocrisy of the Pharisees. He said, ***"Beware ye of the leaven of the Pharisees, which is hypocrisy."*** Don't be affected by it. The hypocrisy they had was, they would live one way where people could see them, and another way in private.

I don't know if you know this or not, but you're not fooling anybody. We know there is a Real You, and there is a Church You. We know most people bring the glorified one to church, and spend the rest of the week being the guy who drives the Corvette, trying to look cool, and making himself out to be someone other than who he really is.

Sometimes *we* don't even know who we are. We think we're the projected person, and then we think we're the person who lives inside the projected person, your self image. Then, there is the third person. The person we *really* are. I'm not sure who he is; only God knows, because you don't really know who you are until the pressure is on. So I look at you and I think, is this the glorified one? Is it the self image? Or am I looking at the real one? Only God can reveal that to me.

In prayer, God will begin to deal with the self image, the person we think we are, and the person we really are. Sometimes, they're not anywhere close to each other. The reason is, in order to be accepted, most of us will move away from who we really are toward our self image, and even toward the glorified image if necessary.

As we grow in prayer, God begins to bring the necessary corrections into our personality. He begins to prune, and some of us don't want to be pruned. We like that dead old branch. We've had it for years. God is going to prune it, and we're going to cry as it falls off.

I don't know what your dead branch might be. You might need to take your TV out in the back yard, shoot the thing, start to pray, and you'll get some real peace for once.

"But it gives me peace of mind when I've had a hard day," you say. I've heard alcoholics say the same thing: the only reason they drink is they need some peace. We all need some peace. Go home and cut the cord off the back of that TV, and begin to pray and listen. You will not only get peace, you'll get your kids back.

THE SIN ROOT

You say, "That's just holiness preaching."

You're right. It will make you whole.

A thief will never steal anything unless he has the opportunity. Jesus said in Matthew 5:28 *"But I say unto you, That whosoever looketh on a woman to lust after her hath committed adultery with her already in his heart."* Now, when is the adultery committed? When you find yourself in bed with someone other than your spouse? No, that is the *fruit* of the sin. The actual sin was the willingness in your heart to commit the sin should the opportunity present itself!

Even though you might never allow the fruit of the sin to grow, you've still sinned. Some of you might get up in the morning, look out in your yard, and be shocked that the tree you'd cut down has grown back. So you run out before anybody sees it and cut it back down to the ground. You think the sin is not in you, because you won't let it produce fruit. You can have the root, or the seed, of sin in you and never let it produce fruit.

Before adultery ever happens in bed, it happens in your heart. The *willingness* is the actual committing of the sin. Sin is first committed in the heart. If you don't believe receiving and partaking of wrong knowledge is sin, the first thing you do when you get to heaven, I want you to find Mr. and Mrs. Adam, and ask them, "Will eating the wrong knowledge cause you trouble?" Their eating the wrong knowledge almost sent us all to hell. It messed up the whole world, and every generation throughout time.

NOT IN SEASON...YET

Now some of you have the tree of sin, but you're not in season; you keep it pruned down, and it won't bear fruit. But what if we throw you on a desert island where there's nobody but you and her, and you don't think you'll ever be rescued? If there is any adultery in you, you'll figure out some way to bring yourself into season. Let enough pressure build against you, and if the seed or root of sin is in there, your tree will bear the fruit of sin.

If a man is willing to steal for any reason, then he's a thief, even though he might not steal because the opportunity never presents itself to do so. If there is any reason you are willing to steal, then thievery is in you.

Don't think you're okay because you pray. It takes more than prayer. If prayer by itself would have worked, Paul would not have had to write the letters. He wrote the letters to make the corrections he received in prayer. It's a whole combination.

SWEEPING OUT THE LEAVEN

How many of you have ever noticed that lying is a defensive form of weaponry? Most of us lie to protect ourselves. But in Luke 12:1 Jesus says **"Beware ye of the leaven of the Pharisees, which is hypocrisy."** The leaven, hypocrisy, is the lie. Listen to this,

For there is nothing covered, that shall not be revealed; neither hid, that shall not be known.

Therefore whatsoever ye have spoken in darkness shall be heard in the light; and that which ye have spoken in the ear in closets shall be proclaimed upon the housetops.

And I say unto you my friends, Be not afraid of them that kill the body, and after that have no more that they can do.

But I will forewarn you whom ye shall fear: Fear him, which after he hath killed hath power to cast into hell; yea, I say unto you, Fear him.

Luke 12:2-5

Sin can be in you if you're willing to let it into your heart. You might not let it bring forth fruit, but if you have the willingness to do it, then it's in you. You need to eradicate it.

Many of us have learned that you reach a point in your life where you have to draw a line, and refuse to go even an inch further. Like David, if you look, you'll get it in your heart, and then you'll start bringing forth fruit.

That's because in your heart you know you are willing to look when nobody is watching. The reason I do my best never to lie is because, if I do, I license the Devil to bring deception back on me. The Devil can move somebody right into your company, he can move somebody right into your church, he can move somebody right into your neighborhood who seems righteous but will cause havoc.

"Be not deceived; God is not mocked; for whatsoever a man soweth, that shall he also reap." (Galatians 6:7) These people might have been with you 20 years, and you can't see the unrighteousness they really walk in because you have the willingness to sow deception yourself. Jesus told me, "I can't send you until you get the willingness to sow the deception out of you."

I refuse to tell a lie because of the consequences. You should also refuse to lie. In the next chapter I'll show you why.

CHAPTER 12
NEVER, NEVER LIE

I had just finished some ministry business and was driving home through Oakridge, Oregon. My son and his girlfriend were in the back seat, my wife was seated next to me, and I was tired. If you know anything about Oregon, you know the police watch you. The city police watch you, the county police watch you, and the state police watch you. I was following a truck up Highway 58. It's about 20 miles to the top of the hill and I'd been following him at a snail's pace for about 10 miles.

Recently God had said to me, "Now I want you to eradicate the lies in your life."

I said, "I don't tell lies."

He said, "The willingness to tell a lie means it's in you and it needs to be out of you." That was really all He said, and I had forgotten about it.

I don't know if you know this or not, but God will not badger you. He didn't jump in the middle of the Garden of Eden and say, "Eve, what are you doing, woman?" If it had been me, I'd have stopped her and said, "Now listen here! Hey, what's going on over there? Hey, let me have your attention for a few moments. Paging Miss Eve. Front garden desk immediately, please." I would have straightened that woman out. Wouldn't you, if you had been God? If God was ever going to straighten anybody out, and make them do something, that was it!

That's what I mean when I say He won't badger you. God will tell you one time, and then it's up to you. If you don't do something, you're in trouble. He won't tell you, over and over. You know, parents should learn this. You tell your kids one time to pick up their clothes, and if they don't do it, then leave the dirty clothes laying there for three months. They'll get the hint.

Anyway, back to this truck I'd been following for the last 10 miles. He was going soooo slow. I had even pulled over once or twice to let the other traffic go by. This truck was barely moving, and I couldn't get around him with any room to spare. Because I had my wife, and my son and his girlfriend with me, I was trying to be a little more cautious in my driving.

Now if I had been by myself, I probably would have taken a chance. But when you have the person you love more than yourself next to you, you start thinking about her. You turn into an old grandma driver.

OPPORTUNITY TAKEN

Finally, I saw my opportunity, and I floored it. I laid it to the floorboard, pedal to the metal. Almost immediately my radar detector went off!

In Oregon, the police have an unwritten policy of always giving you a ticket if they find a radar detector in your car. You can be some older lady who is bleeding to death on your way to the hospital, but if you've got a radar detector, you get the ticket. It's a no excuse policy, and I knew about it.

So when I saw those lights come on, I immediately jerked that radar detector off the windshield, wrapped it up, and told my wife, "Hide it." I began to rub the suction marks off the inside of the windshield.

When the officer got out of the patrol car he came running over and started looking at my windshield, I knew what he was looking for. He was looking for the suction cup marks. My wife said, "What's he doing?" but I didn't say a word. I handed him my license, and he said, "How are you doing, Mr. McFall?"

I said, "Really, I'm not doing too good. Actually, I'm kind of sick," and I was. When I saw those lights, I became sort of queasy, especially when I was going 75 miles per hour. I became sickish, faint at heart. I moaned again, "Oh, I'm not doing too good," I saw he was just standing there, listening to me, and I thought, *"you know this sounds pretty good,"* so I just kept laying it on.

"Well," he says, "just sort of try to slow it down, ok? Let me see your registration." Now I know he has bought my story. I'm starting to get happy inside.

Then my wife reached over and opened the glove box door to get the registration, and the radar detector fell right out onto her lap! The officer jumped back like a scalded dog. "What is that?" He was pointing at the detector in my wife's lap. He began to sort of hop from one foot to the other. "Mr. McFall, what is that?" he asked excitedly.

THE TEST

I thought for a second, and started to turn around to my son to say, "What are you doing with a radar detector in my car?" But the Holy Ghost stopped me right there, and dealt with me, "When the pressure is on," He said, "the real you comes out, because you have a willingness. If you're willing to lie, the Devil will cause some ungodly devil in blue jeans and blue eyes to marry your daughter, and you won't have a clue that he's ungodly."

My moment of truth had come.

I admitted to the officer that I had been using the radar detector when he pulled me over. I took what I had coming to me—an expensive speeding ticket. However, that ticket was a hundred times better than sowing deception. Remember, God won't be mocked, whatever you sow you're going to reap.

When you lie you open the door for deception to come back on you. The Devil will send a Judas into your midst and you won't have a clue they are there. Then, at a critical time in your life, when all hell is breaking loose, and the pressure is on, the Judas will come and kiss you in a moment of betrayal.

You can't afford to lie, unless you want the Devil to tell lies on you. He'll bring it to a multitude of people, and they will discredit you. They will lie about you, and you'll say, "God, what have I done wrong?" It's because you reap what you sow.

THE PLANT NURSERY

I went down to the plant nursery one day and bought a tree. They gave me the right tree, but the wrong price; they shorted themselves $30. When I got home and realized they had mischarged me, Jesus said, "If you steal the Devil will steal from you and when he does, he will steal more than money. He'll steal your health or your children from you, because when you steal he has a right to steal from you and he always takes more than you have."

Now your healing stands in the redemptive rights of Jesus, but if you're willing to take what doesn't belong to you, then you give the Devil the right to take something from you which actually *does* belong to you, like your healing. It happens by opening the door to the Devil through lying. Ephesians 4:27 says, **"Neither give place to the Devil,"** and you give place to the Devil by lying and stealing.

For example, you'll begin to sow money into the Kingdom of God, expecting the promised return on your seed, but you've been stealing something small. Your harvest never reaches you because the Devil steals it before it can get to you. Now he's stealing from you.

Have you noticed how easy it can be to stretch the truth just a little bit? It saves you a lot of hell in the natural, because you're using it as a defensive weapon. In the short run it seems to help you, but in the long run it becomes a weight you have to bear.

Neither lying nor stealing are profitable in the long run because they open the door to Satan to take you captive at *his* will.

BACK TO THE NURSERY

We rushed that tree right back down to the nursery and told them we wanted to pay the right price. You know what? It made them mad. They said, "No, it was our mistake, you can have it."

"Do you own the company?" I asked.

"No."

"Well then, I want to pay the $30."

They thought I was a nut. But I'm telling you, I was more concerned with what was going on in the spiritual realm than I was with $30. If your integrity can be violated, God can't send you where He wants to because, if He does, the Devil will steal your ministry fruit from you.

In fact, 2 Timothy 2:26 says, "Satan can take you captive at his will" (author's paraphrase). You sow deception, the Devil will bring deception back. You steal, then the Devil can steal from you. Truthfully, I'm afraid to take a pencil that doesn't belong to me.

"That sounds like fear, Brother Tim."

Yes, and it's a good thing. The Bible commands us to fear Him. I'm far more concerned with what happens in the spiritual realm than I am the fleshly realm. The problem with sin is, it becomes your master and won't let you obey God. It will trap you with cords so strong only God can get you free.

WHEN DOES SIN OCCUR?

So, when is the sin committed? At the point of your willingness. You might not ever steal unless you were hungry. You might not ever take anything unless you could justify it. The sin begins in your mind with your willingness.

I used to run around with some old boys in Oregon who were so intelligent that, if you were playing chess with them, they could beat you for the next three years. Well, they had me convinced it was okay to go take trees out of the forest and saw them up for personal use. They'd say, "That looks like a good tree there; let's take it home. I mean, after all, this is our tree because the National Forest belongs to us."

Now, I knew something was wrong. It all sounded good and these boys were a lot smarter than I was, but something still wasn't ringing true.

Then they would cut down the tree, load it up, take it home, saw it up, and sell the lumber.

So, I'm thinking, *"Now, he said the tree and the forest belongs to us, we only hire the government to take care of it. It all belongs to us, so we can do what we like with it, right?"* See, people who rob, cheat, and steal always have a logical reason to do what they've done. They become masters of self-justification

FAULTY LOGIC

Jesus asked me, "Do you remember that car that you have?" I said, "Yes," and I knew the other shoe was about to drop.

He said, "Why don't you go sell it without checking with your other half? It's yours, isn't it?"

I immediately saw the flaw in my friend's logic. When you become married you become one. If you go sell that car without checking with the rest of *Us* at home, you're going to be in real trouble when you get there.

I said, "I know, I understand. Just because the trees belong to *Us* doesn't give me the right to go down there and cut one down."

I realized thievery can be justified, and if there is justified theft in your life, God can't use you. You will have trouble with the Devil; you'll pray in the Spirit, you'll sow money, you'll believe God and the Devil will steal it from you anyway. Much of our spiritual frustration has this dynamic at its root.

WHAT YOU DIDN'T KNOW

The problem with all of this is, you don't know you are going to be tested. When I was in Cold Weather Survival Training, I knew I was being tested, so I did a real good job. If somebody would have told me that the test had begun when I put on the radar detector, I would have done much better. As it was, I passed the test as soon as I admitted to the officer I had been using the thing, and I was glad I did...but it was questionable for a few minutes.

Testings and trials aren't something that come on you, they are something you *fall* into (James 1:2 author's paraphrase). They all come as a result of the lust of your flesh. If you're willing to steal, then thievery is in you, even though you might not have stolen for ten years. Jesus told me, "If you are willing to be unforgiving, unforgiveness is in you, and I can't send you until you get it out."

Now what's the problem with unforgiveness? Matthew 18:34-35 tells us.

And his lord was wroth, and delivered him to the tormentors, till he should pay all that was due unto him. So likewise shall my heavenly Father do also unto you, if ye from your hearts forgive not every one his brother their trespasses.

This means every one of them, even the little tiny ones. The willingness to hold unforgiveness will get you in trouble.

THREE KINDS OF DEPRESSION

I had never been depressed until I left home, because of the way I was raised. My mom and dad stuck me in the garden and I worked all day. My father worked at night in the dog mines. They call them "dog mines" because only a dog could stand up in them. They're only 28 to 36 inch high tunnels that ran a mile back up underneath the ground. He would go out there and lay on his back or stomach and load coal all night. Dad would come home the next morning, and want me to go out and work in the garden.

If I had told my dad I didn't want to go to the garden one day, because I "felt sort of depressed," after he had worked all night in the mines, I wouldn't have wanted to be in that house. My dad wouldn't have put up with that.

However, some years later as a young man I was depressed. I didn't know why I was depressed, but I was depressed. When you're depressed, you don't care anymore. That's the first sign of depression. When you hear somebody say things like, "Listen, I don't care anymore. I'm quitting my job, quitting my marriage, and going home, because I don't care any more. I love my wife more than I love myself, but I can't take the hell. I'm leaving." Depression is like something sitting on top of your emotions that won't get off, and you can't struggle out from under it yourself.

There are different forms of depression. A chemical imbalance can cause a depression. A psychiatrist is a regular MD who does another two years of specialized training to make sure, when you come in for counseling or psychoanalysis, he has the ability to determine whether your problem is or is not biological. He wants to make sure there isn't a tumor, or a hormonal imbalance in your body that's causing you to be depressed.

Then there is also self induced depression. Self induced depression is what happened to Eve. Eve had it good, but the Devil told her she could have had it better. She talked herself out of how good she had it, and into sin. Self induced depression happens often when somebody dies. What you do is afflict yourself and won't allow yourself to come out of that self induced depression.

Third, if it's not biological, and it's not self induced, then the only form of depression that remains is spiritual depression. However, before the Devil can seduce you into depression, he has to make you a captivating offer. He must make the offer because he doesn't have a right to put depression on you until you give him permission. How does he get permission? He offers you worry or anxiety. Then he mixes it with fear and hopelessness. If you buy the lie he tries to induce into your thinking, you've opened the door to depression.

I had bought the lie and was depressed

THE WOMAN THE LORD SENT

In the middle of this depression I was at work one day when a lady co-worker came in.

"What's the matter with you?" she asked.

"I'm not feeling too good," I said. "I'm depressed, to tell you the truth. Oh, nobody knows the hell I've seen."

I couldn't tell you now what it was that had me depressed, but it sure seemed bad at the time. I sure didn't know why in the world I was spilling my guts to this lady.

She talked to me and, after a bit, when she saw she wasn't getting anywhere, she left. Within minutes, whatever was on me, all of a sudden, felt like it had jumped off! I hopped up and shouted, "Ohh, I feel good!" It felt like an adrenaline rush or something; my body chemistry just went wild. *What happened to me?* I wondered. *It's that woman, she did something to me!* So I ran and caught her right before she got to her car.

"What did you do to me?" I demanded.

"You had a big old Devil sitting on your head." she said.

"I didn't either!" I protested.

"It was there," she said, "I told it to leave and it did. Don't you feel better?"

"I do, I really do feel better."

Sure enough, her prayer had delivered me from spiritual depression.

Now if I'm depressed, I *know* I'm depressed. So the Devil is smart enough to leave me alone. You're smart enough to know if you wake up and you're depressed, the Devil's been working on you. You know you're under attack, so you'll call somebody for help.

Another door Satan looks to gain entrance through is the door of unforgiveness. He'll find the offense you're holding and launch an attack through that open door.

CLOSE THE DOOR OF UNFORGIVENESS

What does the tormentor do if he knows you are wise to his attack of spiritual depression? He bypasses you, and jumps all over your children. Because you got up and you prayed all morning and felt pretty good, you thought everything was okay. But he's still been turned loose because of your unforgiveness.

Not only is he working on your children, but he's working on your ministry and working on your church. He's even working on your job, but because you feel good, you think he's not working at all. He's smart enough to know that if he attacks you directly, you'll fight him off.

When you open the door through unforgiveness, he leaves you alone, and goes to work on your children or on your co-workers, making them act ugly. Your church can also come under this unforgiveness licensed attack. He knows he can't shake you with a direct attack, but if he can hurt your little ones, he shakes you.

If one of my little ones has been hurt, I can't get a moment of peace until we get rid of that thing. When they hurt, I hurt. But let me tell you, the Devil is still being loosed.

Now, I wouldn't go down to the store and steal something, because I know that would let the Devil get a hold of me. But James 3:16 says, *"For where envying and strife is, there is confusion and every evil work."*

Now what do you consider evil? Jesus told me, "You close that door and stop the tormentor by repenting and getting rid of your *willingness* to commit sin." You have to make a decision not to look over that banister and go "Uh-huh..." You have to make a decision you're not going to lie, and you don't care what happens to you. No matter what you have to give up, if God is your source, you'll get it back, and more.

IT'S YOUR TURN NOW

Will you, this day, come to repentance? Turn from lying, stealing, lust and unforgiveness? God is calling you to repentance, to change your heart. If you're willing to repent of the willingness to commit sin, you will see a change in your life. It will take a commitment to say, "Yes Jesus, I'm willing to close the door to sin, and lie no more, steal no more, and lust no more. I will not hold offenses or harbor bitterness or unforgiveness. I am willing to change." James chapter 1 says if you will ask for wisdom, God will give it to you. However, He will only give it if you are willing to ask in faith (author's paraphrase). "In faith" means you are willing to change when the wisdom comes. It begins with repentance. Say, "God, I repent, I ask for forgiveness. I am willing to change. **I close the door to the Devil.**"

* * *

When you have made the decision to close that door, please write me and tell me about it. We'd also love to hear your praise reports. Our ministry has materials specifically designed to help you keep that door closed.

May God bless you.

For a list of books and audio tapes by
Timothy McFall
or for other information, please write:

Timothy McFall Ministries
P.O. Box 1902
Klamath Falls, Oregon 97601
(541) 882-8668